IN THE
BEGINNING

IN THE BEGINNING

A Christian Parent's Guide
to Building Confidence
in the Early Years

JOHN KAITES

RIVER GROVE
BOOKS

This book is intended as a reference volume only. It is sold with the understanding that the publisher and author are not engaged in rendering any professional services. The information given here is designed to help you make informed decisions.

Published by River Grove Books
Austin, TX
www.rivergrovebooks.com

Distributed by River Grove Books

Design and composition by Greenleaf Book Group and Mimi Bark
Cover design by Greenleaf Book Group and Mimi Bark
Cover images used under license from ©Shutterstock.com/Evgeny Atamanenko

Scripture quotations marked (NIV) are taken from the *Holy Bible, New International Version* (NIV). Copyright © 1973, 1978, 1984, 2011 by Biblica, Inc. Used by permission of Zondervan. All rights reserved worldwide. The "NIV" and "New International Version" are trademarks registered in the United States Patent and Trademark Office by Biblica, Inc.

Scripture quotations marked (ESV) are from *The ESV Bible* (*The Holy Bible, English Standard Version*). Copyright © 2001 by Crossway, a publishing ministry of Good News Publishers. Used by permission. All rights reserved.

Publisher's Cataloging-in-Publication data is available.

Print ISBN: 978-1-63299-586-5

eBook ISBN: 978-1-63299-587-2

First Edition

To my wife, Ann, who, when it came to raising our sons, Alex and Jacob, was—and still is—an amazing mother, teacher, motivator, partner, and team player

CONTENTS

INTRODUCTION

After giving the Sermon on the Mount, Jesus speaks in Matthew 7:24–27 about the importance of building a strong foundation in our lives. He said if we listen to His words and follow them, our lives are like a house built on rock. The wind will blow, and the storms will come, but because we have a strong foundation built on rock rather than sand, we will always stand firm. This, He said, is wise, and He offered this instruction because He wants what's best for us.

God's teachings are themselves foundational to helping us live a life that pleases and honors Him, while also allowing us to be at our fullest potential. When we have a strong foundation, we have hope, peace, and joy. We live meaningfully, purposefully, and confidently.

As parents, we want this for our children too. We do our best to give them a solid foundation in life so that they can grow stronger physically, mentally, emotionally, and spiritually. We want them to be able to stand tall with confidence, to know who they are, and to live fully.

When we think about our lives now, we likely recognize that we have certain approaches, feelings, and responses to situations that are driven by our own personalities. How we tackle a problem, move past a barrier, or work toward a goal might be unique to us and bring about either positive or negative outcomes. But what many of us don't realize is that the ways we think and act now are significantly influenced by repetitive patterns that formed in our heads from when we were born until we were around the age of seven. Those patterns continue into adulthood to drive much of our success or failure, and they dictate how we approach and solve the fundamental problems life can bring our way.

Certainly, after age seven, we mold, shape, and refine our minds in response to the good and bad that we experience in life; we grow and adapt, and development continues through our teen years. But this book specifically focuses on how the first eight years of our life (from birth through age seven) create the foundation of our subconscious mind. These beginning years, with their unique developmental milestones, are critical, and I believe that with a better understanding of how to parent in these early years, we can help build a strong foundation for our kids. If we were building a house, we wouldn't choose a foundation made of sand but would want the sturdiest and most solid foundation available, right? *In the Beginning* is about providing you with guidance, research, a biblical perspective, and firsthand experience as a parent, so you can establish this strong foundation for your kids right from the start.

As parents, we have immense power to influence our children's development and also the amazing privilege of helping our kids become all God has created them to be. What we do amplifies either positively or negatively in their minds from the first day they're conceived. Our habits and emotional, physical, and mental well-being transfer to our children's own emotional, physical, mental, and spiritual health.

Research shows that 97 percent of everything we do is subconscious.[1] Humans are primarily subconscious beings, and while you may think you control your thoughts and emotions, you probably only see and feel the finished product of the thoughts and feelings that have already filtered through your subconscious mind.

Between the ages of zero and seven, the mind develops rapidly and uniquely, so much so that even the simplest repetitive encouragement can prime a child's brain and allow them to feel the kind of safety and security that can launch them toward a healthy life, one in which they dwell in authentic confidence. It's humbling to realize that most of a human being's "I can do this" mentality forms during these early stages of childhood. It may be even more humbling to recognize that most of the "I am not good enough to do this" mentality is also formed during these ages.

This book will help you understand that everything your child sees, hears, feels, and senses in this small window of time becomes part of the subconscious story they will likely tell themselves for the rest of their life. Their subconscious is a critical part of their emotional and physical foundation as a human being. We as parents have the opportunity in these beginning years to understand how our kids are growing and actually input data points into their brains in a way that allows them to flourish. A healthy, happy child with authentic confidence possesses a deep inner-subconscious knowledge that no matter what challenges they may face, they will be okay. Their mind will be full of the truth about who they really are, and their identity will be secure, largely unaffected by the lies that the world can tell them. Our authentically confident kids will understand that they are fully known and loved by you and by God. They will know the truth: that they are good enough and capable enough, loved and loveable. They will feel that they are bolstered by God's grace, hope, peace, and strength, and in this, they will be intentional in their choices and unafraid to take on the challenges of life.

In the Beginning is designed to give you the knowledge you need to help your child grow a healthy, confident brain and minimize the possibility that they will develop an insecure, fearful brain that hinders them in life. Each of the seven chapters focuses on the corresponding year in a child's life, providing insights that will allow you to better navigate your way as a parent through the first seven years. Chapter 1 covers birth through the end of age one, Chapter 2 covers through the end of age two, and the remaining chapters provide the relevant information you'll need for each subsequent year until age seven. The chapters also end with a short prayer to frame the information and allow you to connect with God on how to implement your newfound knowledge.

If you're a first-time parent, a grandparent, a caregiver, or a foster or adoptive parent, this book can help you. Though this book isn't intended to serve as an exhaustive resource on the first seven years of a child's life—and I recognize that every experience is different—it does highlight information that, if used correctly, can become the sturdy building blocks of a strong foundation in a child's life.

I once drew a graph on the back of a napkin to illustrate the big picture of parenting. Our children are entirely dependent on us at birth, and they rely on us for everything. However, if we do our job well as parents, each year we raise them to become more independent and more authentically confident, equipping them with what they need to succeed and live a good life beyond their teen years.

The graph, as follows, shows a healthy trajectory of growth, with a child becoming more and more independent with every year. By the age of eighteen, the child should be fully capable of being independent, as they will be equipped with the skills, knowledge, and experience they need to continue through life in a confident and fruitful way without your assistance. The implication this has for us as parents is that we are actively and intentionally coaching our kids with this goal in mind. We will love and guide them but with each year, we need to give up more and more control so that our kids can practice and learn how to be independent. This doesn't mean we care less. It means we recognize that to be truly authentically confident and living life at their fullest potential, our kids need us to give them room to grow.

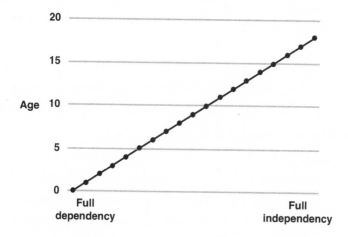

When I coach new parents on the strategies and tactics of raising authentically confident children, I emphasize studying to be a great parent. If you think about it, being a parent is the most important lasting legacy that we leave on this earth. How we raise our children will affect generations of our descendants and impact the world exponentially over time. Interestingly, we spend years studying for our careers or training for our vocational futures, but more often than not, parenting seems left up to our own experience or initiative—what we've observed, read, been told, or tried. We don't necessarily have degrees in parenting, and sometimes, we're not even positive we're doing it right. The result often winds up as a subconscious transfer of our own personal strengths and weaknesses to our children and, beyond that, to their children. I recommend learning all you can about parenting kids in these crucial beginning years of their life, adding the insights in this book to your parenting toolbox.

In the days before the internet, my wife and I made it a practice to visit our local library and look at all the books pertaining to the ages of our children. Over time, we developed the practice of reading five age-relevant books per year, usually around our kids' birthdays. This gave us a brief but helpful, insightful look into the future year with each of our kids by removing some of the developmental surprises, allowing us to better anticipate what was to come, and providing us with some proven strategies and tactics we knew we would be able to use if needed.

Consider this book as offering a similar approach. You can skip ahead to the chapter and age that applies to your child, or reread a particular chapter around a birthday so you can prepare for the next year. I encourage you to read through the entire book first and then to later return to find what you need, so the information is fresher in your mind. I pray and expect your life and your child's will be dramatically benefited when you know where they are in their development and how you can be intentional about growing their brain in a loving, encouraging way.

God knew exactly what He was doing in creating us in the way He did. Our brains are miraculous, and our children are miracles themselves. My hope is that in going through this book, you will feel more confident as a parent, and your child will thrive as a result. Let us help our kids live free of fear, worry, or insecurity so that they may be fully and authentically confident. And let us be humble stewards of the amazing kids God has entrusted to us, as we seek to bring out their best and raise them in a way that is all about His goodness and glory. This is my vision for you and the reason for this book.

Chapter 1

AGE ZERO THROUGH ONE: A NEW LIFE

For you created my inmost being; you knit me together
in my mother's womb. I praise you because I am fearfully
[morally reverent] and wonderfully made; your works are
wonderful, I know that full well.

—Psalm 139:13–14 (NIV)

The Bible tells us that we are morally reverent and wonderfully made. Some translations of this verse say that we're "fearfully" made, which comes from the Old Testament Hebrew word *yare*, and communicates reverence, awe, respect, and honor in this context. That we're fearfully made and morally reverent from the moment we're created carries some deep meaning and weight. It implies that we should have a reverent fear and praise for the God who made us. The Hebrew word for "wonderfully" is *palah*, meaning distinct, set apart, distinguished, or marvelous. To me, these are some powerful words to use when talking about our lives, aren't they?

From the moment a child is conceived, their brain, like their body, begins to grow and be knit together. Six weeks after conception, the baby starts to move. By three months, the baby begins to swallow, stretch, and suck their thumb. God has knit every cell, fiber, and tissue together—what a miracle the way a baby develops in a mother's womb. Research tells us that before birth, the cerebral cortex—the thin neural tissue that covers most of our brain and is associated with determining our motor function, sensory processing, intelligence, personality, use of language, sense of touch, and ability to plan and organize—is already formed.[1] All this and more is taking shape in a child's brain before they see the light of day. We are, as the Bible says, morally and wonderfully made creations in the eyes of God before we even take our first breath of air.

Recognizing that God entrusts parents with these amazingly created human beings, how do we know the best way to take care of them, nurture them, and foster their growth? How do we understand what they most need, when we're supposed to provide it, and what's going through their brains?

When you first learned you were pregnant, you probably experienced a flood of emotions, including joy and excitement mixed with some worry and fear about the responsibility of taking care of a life. (I know I did!) You likely visited the doctor, planned and prepared, thought about what your child would be like and how you would be as a parent. If you're like most parents, you probably also felt a desire to keep your child safe and happy no matter what, providing for them and setting them up for a good life.

To be the best parents we can be, especially for our newborns, I believe we need to be the best possible versions of ourselves. Psalm 1 says that those who meditate and delight in the things of the Lord are like trees planted firmly by streams of living water. If we love and seek out God in all we do, including parenting, we'll be like a well-watered tree; our leaves will not wither, we can be constantly refreshed, and we will yield fruit. God willing, this book can be a stream of living water for you. Things will not go perfectly on your parenting journey, particularly if you're new to it and just starting out, but if you are planted in Jesus, you will always have a new day, a fresh start, a bright beginning, and most importantly, a miracle from God. My prayer is that this chapter can provide truths and insights that help you better understand the brain development and particular needs of your child in their first years.

Newborn and One-Year-Old Brain Activity: The Spongy Brain

Now for some of the science behind the happenings in your child's brain during the newborn through the one-year-old stage. On the surface, it probably looks like all your newborn does so far is sleep, eat, poop, wiggle, giggle, cry, and scream. They are a small person in an enormous world full of new and strange sounds, smells, colors, and sensations.

Try to picture if you, yourself, were suddenly thrust into an alien world for the first time. You wouldn't understand what you're seeing, hearing, or feeling. Maybe everything in this unfamiliar world seems too bright and loud to you, and you were used to something darker and calmer where you came from. You're probably uncertain, don't know what's going on, and may be a little frightened.

To a baby, everything is new. They don't understand everything in the same way you do at this point, but they are receiving and absorbing all of it. Think of a newborn's brain as a tiny sponge in these first crucial months.

According to an article on children and brain development prepared by the University of Maine, a baby's brain contains 100 billion neurons at birth, which is "roughly as many nerve cells as there are stars in the Milky Way, and almost all the neurons the brain will ever have."[2] That's a lot of neurons. The fact that a baby already has most of these from the start also says something about the complexity of their brain. If, on the surface, it doesn't seem like your baby is doing a lot more than eating or sleeping, rest assured that there is more going on—and it's quite impressive.

Neurons—networks of specialized nerve cells that use signals to communicate with one another—are important. They fire electronic and chemical charges through synaptic nerve endings to other neurons, and these messages serve as the basis of learning and memory."[3] The active neurons inside your baby's brain react to everything happening in the outside world and form synapses that can create wanted or unwanted patterns. Your baby is learning, remembering, and processing patterns from the environment and stimuli around them. Given that you, as parents, are a huge part of their world, what you do, say, and expose your baby to is being received, and their brain is working it out.

At birth, each neuron has roughly 2,500 synapses, which are like tiny roadways in the brain, and these grow in number to around

15,000 by the time your child is two or three years old.[4] Research from Harvard shows that more than one million new neural connections form every second in the first few years of your baby's life.[5] These connections are where all thought comes from. Considering that your baby's brain contains around 100 billion neurons, you can imagine that at any given time, your baby is absorbing and processing faster than you can imagine. Because of these neurons, your baby doesn't miss a moment. Everything that happens to them internally and externally affects their development.

This, to me, means that everything counts. If, as parents, we pour love, safety, and security into our interactions with our baby, that's one million connections per second that make a positive impact in our child's brain. But if the external stimuli a child receives consistently involve fear, distress, or insecurity, that's one million connections per second that can have an adverse effect on their development. Remember that a child's brain is a sponge in these first years. Stress and trauma can have long-term negative consequences for the newborn brain, whereas loving interactions can stimulate positive brain growth.

I encourage you to speak words of life and love over your child always but especially during these early stages. Repeat to your child how much you, as parents, and Jesus love them. Tell them they are smart, talented, wise, honest, kind, strong, compassionate, caring, friendly, creative, and a problem-solving leader. Even if you think they can't understand and you feel a bit silly at first, say these things from the day your baby is born and for the rest of their lives. Your child and their children will reap the benefits for generations.

And don't only speak love but *show* love to them. It is in what you do, how you make yourself available, and what they see in your facial expressions. If they feel loved, their neurons will communicate that to one another, and their synapses will ensure this message keeps getting sent.

There's much more that all this involves, of course, but I marvel at the beauty and complexity of the newborn's and one-year-old's brain. They are learning every moment. Physiologically, God made it so, and how amazing to think that He designed us like this for our best and for His glory.

We are indeed fearfully and wonderfully made.

Confidence Building Blocks

Knowing that your baby's brain, in these first years, is acting as a sponge, what are some things you can do to help them develop in a positive, healthy way? How can you establish a firm foundation for them and play a role in shaping their brain so that they are happy, capable, and authentically confident human beings? As we've seen, a baby's brain is processing, learning, and remembering at all times. I believe that even at this young age, they can experience confidence and security, which makes them better equipped to grow, thrive, and become more resilient.

As a parent, you have, at the most basic level, the responsibility of doing three things simultaneously for your child: nourish their body, nourish their mind, and nourish their soul. I'll briefly touch on these in the paragraphs that follow before getting into some of the actual confidence building blocks for your baby.

NOURISH THEIR BODY

We know that babies rely on us for food and the right kinds of sustenance to be able to grow at their best. A malnourished or underfed body (and brain!) cannot properly develop. To raise a healthy, happy, confident child, we must learn the kinds of nutrition they'll need at every key stage to be physically strong.

Your baby will also crave your touch. Julie Greicius, in a piece written for Stanford Medicine, discusses the benefits of touch for babies throughout their infancy and beyond, citing enhanced awareness, better sleep, improved neurological function, and reduced fussiness as just a few of the advantages.[6] Hold and hug your baby. Encourage the development of their motor skills as they grow. Make sure they feel you're for them and will respond to their needs. Taking care of your baby physically sets them up for a strong, successful start in life, which contributes to their ability to feel good and be authentically confident.

NOURISH THEIR MIND

I also want to stress the importance of providing good mental stimulation for babies in this age range. There are countless studies that have found that engaging a baby's brain, especially when done in concert with the development of their motor skills and sensory perception, brings about healthy gains. The Centers for Disease Control and Prevention (CDC) tells us, "Nurturing care for the mind is critical for brain growth."[7] But what does this look like?

You can start by simply providing positive, language-enriched engagement and affirmation for your child. They may only seem to be making baby noises, but you can respond by using kind but exaggerated facial expressions, drawing out your vowels, using sing-song speech, keeping your pitch high yet gentle, and repeating words and sounds; using "parentese," as people often call it, can help your baby begin to learn and comprehend language, something that stimulates their mental growth.

You can also play simple, developmentally appropriate games with them that involve the use of their hands, or show them colorful toys or books. If you capture their interest and attention, you allow their neurons to fire. Remember: your baby's brain is a sponge, and everything counts.

Conversely, if a baby is not stimulated enough, this can have a detrimental effect. Neuroscientist Audrey van der Meer, a professor at the Norwegian University of Science and Technology (NTNU), has used EEG technology for many years to study the brain activity of babies and found that synapses that are not stimulated are lost. Her research shows that "if the new synapses that are formed in the brain are not being used, they disappear as the child grows up and the brain loses some of its plasticity."[8]

To raise a healthy, happy child with a strong mind, we need to optimize the time we have for mental stimulation, recognizing that this window of opportunity from zero to one is hugely important. I'll add that a healthy mind is one that is primed for authentic confidence.

NOURISH THEIR SOUL

Nourishing your child's soul calls for a prayerful approach because it speaks to that part of us that responds to God's presence. It has to do with who we are as an individual at our very essence and our connection with God's Spirit. But how do you help your baby grow in this regard?

I humbly submit that as parents, we protect our children's mental and emotional health and provide spiritual affirmation. We want to make sure they feel well taken care of, know that we love and respect them for who they are at their very essence, and—in whatever way a baby can—observe that we submit to God because we, ourselves, need Him. At the end of the day, we have been entrusted to love, care for, and raise our kids, but God is the only one who can touch their souls in that way. As parents of newborns, we can pray that God would nourish their souls, growing them in beauty, strength, hope, and confidence on the inside. We should always focus on who they are and how special they are, and they should feel seen, heard, and cherished by us and by God. We should be attuned to their needs and intentional about how we interact with them, always looking for ways to connect and encourage. Let us endeavor to guide our bundles of joy and ensure that their spongy brain and the soul God gave them are getting everything they need.

The practical, everyday ways in which you might nourish your baby's body, mind, and soul are endless, and I love that this journey of parenting has to be unique to you, your child, and the way God created each of you to be. Our situations, sensibilities, and strengths are different, and there really is no one size fits all. The confidence building blocks that follow will give you a solid start with your baby in their first years, but know that there is freedom in how you apply them to the relationship dynamic you have with your child.

MAKE THEM FEEL SAFE

The ability to feel safe, secure, and stable is important to any person's well-being. For your baby, the emotions that are attached to a sense of safety begin in utero and extend into the first years of their life. For them to develop physically, mentally, emotionally, and spiritually after birth and beyond that, they need you, as the primary influence in their life, to provide this for them. Your child is entirely reliant on you for safety, which means you have a direct influence on the degree of happiness, health, and confidence they feel.

When children know that they are safe from physical, mental, or emotional harm, their bodies can feel relaxed, and they have more focus and mental bandwidth. The reassurance we provide as parents can go a long way toward building their sense of safety and confidence. Babies, with their spongy brains and billions of neurons, are constantly reading our cues, so the way we smile in response to their actions, calm or soothe them with our voices, or hold them gently contributes to their overall feeling of safety.

Don't underestimate the power you have to influence your baby. I saw a video online in which a dad, holding his baby, used his hand to make a loud noise on a door. The baby, not knowing that his father had made the noise on purpose, looked to his dad to see what was going on. The dad smiled to the person holding the camera and pretended that the sound had happened because the child's head had bumped into the door. He comforted the child, which caused the child to immediately reach for his own head and start crying, even though he really hadn't felt a thing. This idea went on to become a TikTok challenge, and I find it fascinating that in video after video, simply because of a parent's dramatic reaction, the child thinks something bad has actually happened and responds to the emotions rather than the reality of the situation. While the videos themselves are intended to be harmless and humorous, I think they also point to the fact that our kids look to us for emotional cues, and how we make them feel can color their perception.

As your baby grows, consider your interactions and responses. Are you meeting their everyday needs in a way that makes them feel calm, safe, and confident in your love? If they are hurt or upset, are you attentive and reassuring, keeping the emotions of the situation in check for them? Often, your child's reaction will be in direct response to your reaction. If you overreact or communicate that a problem is bigger than it is, they may feel fear or worry. But if you respond calmly, capably, and positively, assuming that's the appropriate level of response for the situation, their spongy brain will take this in and pass it between all those neurons. Learning happens from this. A resilient, secure, confident brain develops from this.

We can also help our child feel safe by ensuring that they have a safe environment. Make their home a place they enjoy and find comfort in, let them know that you are present there, and surround them with stimuli like toys and books that are pleasant and evoke positive emotions. If you are out with your baby, be sensitive to times when they seem overwhelmed or overstimulated. And make sure they also feel safe with the people you allow to interact with them.

Prayer is important too. We have a huge influence on our kids' lives, but we're only human and can't control every situation. God, who is all-knowing, all-powerful, and omnipresent, has your baby's best interests at heart, and you can ask Him to keep your child safe and help them feel secure. Be constantly praying for and over your infant, including using words of love, warmth, and encouragement in their presence. You can pray for their growth, their future, their feelings, and their sense of well-being. You can pray for their protection and for God's favor, goodness, and blessing in their life. The love they feel should be a refuge for them, so that they feel secure enough to grow, try things, and venture into the next stage of their development.

How can you tell if your baby feels safe? How can you understand them, especially if they're pre-verbal? Remember that even if your baby appears only to be looking cute with a bit of drool dripping down their chin, their brain is actually processing everything. When a baby feels safe, they sleep well, engage with you, play, smile, and explore. They will feel secure enough to cry, knowing that you'll be there to meet their needs. And they'll be more quickly and easily comforted by you because they trust you.[9]

To help your baby grow happily and confidently, make them feel safe. Send messages of safety and security to their brain, and their neurons will keep this feeling going.

GIVE THEM ROOM TO TRY, LEARN, AND GROW

I've found that active play is excellent for confidence-building. At this young age, your child depends on and needs you, but playtime can also challenge them to solve problems. If your almost-one-year-old is trying to place a square peg in a round hole and becomes frustrated, it's okay to give them hands-on support, but as you help, allow them to be the one to maneuver the peg into the correct hole. Then celebrate the victory together because your face is the first place they'll look to for approval. Your encouragement and enthusiasm are something they will process and remember, and they will feel confident about trying more things the next time the opportunity presents itself.

Instead of developing an "I'm not good enough" or "I can't do it" mentality after something doesn't work out, babies can instead recognize "I am capable" when they succeed at a task or gain a new skill. That small victory of finding the correct hole for the square block is significant, and their neurons will latch on to that. As parents, let's fan the flame of excitement in them and make sure they sense our approval. The more we can provide activity-based support to challenge them and introduce new experiences, the more small victories they will have. I recommend choosing tasks that are just hard enough to be interesting to them but still within their ability to master. If your child has figured out all the buttons on one toy, next time offer them a toy that they can engage with differently, ideally one that builds on their new abilities.

Allow for repetition with games and tasks too. This offers a great way for your child to learn, practice new skills, and continue to develop in confidence. Your child will probably want to do certain kinds of activities over and over and *over* again because the activities are interesting and fun. From a brain development standpoint, repetitive acts are essential for a child in this age range. Your baby needs to practice skills to learn them, just like we do for things that are new to us. Correctly grasping a toy, clapping their hands, or placing a circular peg in a round hole—again and again—is your child's way of achieving mastery, and each new skill learned is a stepping stone toward the next skill. If they feel like they're good at a particular task, they may be motivated to keep trying it. Sure, some of this repetition may become monotonous for parents from time to time, but keep your child's growth and development front of mind, encouraging them and showing them active support. Celebrate their small victories, find ways to make individual tasks more interesting or fun for yourself, and enjoy this special time when you child is at this age. They'll be entering the next stage of development before you know it.

ESTABLISH ROUTINES THEY CAN COUNT ON

Along with the previous confidence building blocks in this chapter, I encourage you to establish routines for your baby. This will create a shape to their day that they can anticipate and expect. Though they may not explicitly recognize that they're following a routine, providing consistency and structure builds comfort and predictability into their life and allows them to feel safe. Infants go through many phases quickly, so you'll want to adjust your routines to their sleeping and eating cycles in a way that makes sense, but as they grow, they'll come to understand through the consistency you establish that they can count on and trust you and others. With routines built into the family dynamic and household rhythm, they'll learn what's expected of them, be able to anticipate how you will respond to them, and become familiar with how to function and behave in a given situation.

Routine, according to an article in *Parents*, can help a child in their first years begin to understand object permanence, a concept that means they know people or objects exist even if they cannot immediately see them. It also enables a child to begin to grasp the idea of sequencing. "By the one-year mark, your little one will begin to understand that bath time comes after dinner, shoes go on after socks," the article reads.[10]

Most of us, including adults, need some sort of structure in our life. Without it, we can experience a sense of unease or be directionless. Routine allows us a way to experience a degree of control in a situation and helps us move forward. Setting up routines now can help lay a solid foundation for life patterns that will serve them well beyond their first years. You won't be able to schedule every last detail with a baby—flexibility is important too—but setting up consistent rituals for meals, play, and sleep can be healthy for them. This, I've found, helps with the growth and development of a happy, confident, well-adjusted child.

BE A GOOD ROLE MODEL

Because we, as parents, spend the most time with our babies, we are probably their most important role models. Knowing that their brains work like sponges in their first years, we have a tremendous opportunity to imprint their young minds with the values and behaviors we hope they'll exhibit once they're older. Our infants learn by observing us, watching how we interact with them and others, hearing how we come across in tone, and noticing what actions we take. Research on the development of self-confidence in children under twelve months of age shows that "babies are quite skilled at interpreting our facial expression, tone of voice, and even the level of tension in our body as we hold them."[11] It's incredible to me that babies can take in so much, even sensing our mood when we hold them. We have tremendous influence, whether positive or negative, and I believe we need to be intentional about how we live our lives and model behavior.

We should consider our attitudes and actions; make sure our behavior lines up with our words; demonstrate kindness, patience, compassion, peace, and respect; and seek to have positive, gracious interactions with others. We should be honest, whether we think our infants recognize this or not. We should love big, listen well, be present, and show what faith looks like. How well do we respond in frustrating situations? How much do we show that we love and respect our spouses? How do we celebrate victories? Our children are impressionable, and they will copy our behaviors and respond according to the feelings we convey. Let's demonstrate the values we want our children to adopt, nurturing them and showing them what it looks like to be positive, capable, confident human beings. We can engage their neurological pathways and model behaviors that will make an impact now and also leave a lifelong impression.

READ TO THEM

When my boys were young, my career at the time made it so that it was difficult for me to be around as much as I wanted to be. On Mondays through Thursdays, I would see them first thing in the morning and only again when it was time to tuck them into bed at night. I had the busyness of work and tasks I hoped to accomplish, and I constantly felt like I had no extra time. I knew I was being pulled in different directions, but I didn't want to miss what was most important.

It occurred to me that my young infant in those days just wanted to hear my voice and be with me. I spent some weeks making it a priority to read to and spend time with him. I read to him from Dr. Seuss and other children's books, as well as a book on integrity and entrepreneurship that my friend and mentor had written.[12] The book from my friend wasn't intended for kids, but my infant son heard my voice and felt my presence as I read from its pages. I read with him to open up the neural pathways in his mind and help him receive the ideas so that he could grow in positive, encouraging, and confident ways. I doubt, at that age, he would have remembered any of the book directly, but I believe some of the time we spent together in that book and the closeness we experienced *were* input into his brain.

Though, in those years, I primarily incorporated children's books into our readings, the main messages of everything I read to him were in his subconscious mind, there to be used in the future. I know the positive input that reading has had on both of my sons, who are now grown. The books we read together were reflected in their excellent grades throughout their academic careers, in their positive character traits, and even in their choices of study in college (both business majors!). I believe, especially where our subconscious is concerned, that everything circles back to the way we live our lives, even at the youngest age.

With your own young children, I think it's hugely important to read them books that are positive and make them better people—books that elevate them and those around them. Read them books designed especially for them and their current level of development, but also read them things that seem beyond their current levels of capability: your favorite Bible verses or success or self-help books meant for adults. I believe the information and the heart and spirit behind these more advanced books can still get through, especially if you're engaging with your child in a loving, connected way. So hold them in love and provide them with input for their spongy brains to take in.

As the parent of a newborn or one-year-old, you are taking on one of the greatest responsibilities and miracles that life offers us as humans. No amount of money, fame, or success is more important than the role of a mom or dad in a child's life. So love your child with everything you've got, and take care of your growing family. And do this prayerfully. If God is at the center of your life and your parenting, you will not fail. He is infinitely wiser and a better Father than any parent can be. Though life will not be perfect, He is, so you can look to him to provide hope, help, direction, and inspiration.

I hope the ideas and insights in this chapter will guide you toward raising an authentic, confident young child. If you build on these concepts, using them as a foundation, your baby will enter the next stage of their development already in a good place.

PRAYER

Lord, you made my child just the way you wanted them to be. Please give me the wisdom to better understand the beautiful uniqueness of their subconscious mind and help fill their brain with the fullness and goodness of your love and authentic confidence. I pray for every synapse and neuron to come together around healthy love-based thoughts and that you would help them to feel safe and secure. Please help me with any fear and insecurity I experience in parenting my child and give me the ability to trust and lean into your amazing grace, love, and strength. I cannot parent without you, and I thank you that you not only know what's best but also go ahead of me into the next stage of development of my child. In Jesus's name, amen.

Chapter 2

AGE TWO: ENTERING THE TODDLER YEARS

―――――――――∞―――――――――

Children are a heritage from the LORD, offspring a reward
from him. Like arrows in the hands of a warrior are children
born in one's youth. Blessed is the man whose quiver is full
of them. They will not be put to shame when they contend
with their opponents in court.

—Psalm 127:3-5 (NIV)

In the psalms, we learn that our kids are a heritage and reward
sent directly from the Lord. They're not rewards for our good
deeds, we come to understand, but gifts to us because God is gracious and wants to bless us and others through our children. As our
heritage, they are entrusted to us to raise, and we have a responsibility to bring them up in the best way possible to honor God and help
them live the life they were uniquely created for.

The psalmist describes children as arrows in the hands of a war-rior. I love this powerful and poignant analogy. Our children are like arrows that we, as parents, can guide and direct. They strengthen us as a family and make us better and more secure. Blessed is the man (or parent!) with a quiver (or house!) full of children, Psalm 127 tells us. If ever a time of judgment or hardship falls on us, family is always there to contend on our behalf.

I believe that our children are one of the greatest rewards we could ever receive from our heavenly Father. As "arrows" that God has placed in our hands and lives, our job is to keep them safe, hold them steady, and then launch them when it's time. I've found that some people will take Psalm 127 to mean that our primary task is to prepare our children like arrows and fire them off into the world to share the gospel, feed the hungry, help the disadvantaged, and live out the legacy they were made for. This is all very true and good, but I notice at the same time that the man whose quiver is full of them is simply blessed, and the passage does not necessarily yet describe the arrows as having been fired. Whatever stage our kids are in—they could very well be on the other side of the world one day—I think this psalm reminds us that it's a tremendous blessing just to keep our kids close in heart. We will raise and equip them to live in the world, but we also need to ensure that we forge deep relationships with them, love them, sharpen them, teach them to be strong, and help them understand that we'll always be there for them. This is how we bring up a confident, independent human who can operate at their fullest potential in any context or setting.

Your two-year-old is part of your heritage and an incredible gift. The stage of development they've reached is one in which they're bus-ily walking, running, and climbing, discovering they can move about on their own in the world around them. Their vocabulary is increasing every day, and they are able to talk and identify all sorts of items. They can distinguish between and sort colors, shapes, and objects. And they may even be demonstrating a readiness for potty training.

Raising a two-year-old comes with its own joys and challenges. Your toddler is full of energy, trying new skills and finding out what they're capable of. Their ability to engage in different activities is impressive, and they're probably figuring out how to push boundaries (and buttons!) as they become more independent. You may notice that they seem defiant or difficult at times and are more prone to temper tantrums.

In this chapter, I'll discuss some of the changes your child is going through during this stage and show you how understanding those changes can allow you to better guide your child to a place of love, patience, and confidence. We'll also talk about the reality and myth of the "terrible twos" and what it looks like to establish healthy patterns and habits for your toddler that will enable them to thrive.

Parenting a child in this stage of development, as in any stage, takes faithfulness, wisdom, and prayer. Age two requires special energy and attention, but I hope that the insights in this chapter will give you the ability to fully enjoy this year and bring out the best in your child, yourself, and your family.

Two-Year-Old Brain Activity: Mobility, Memory, and Me

Your little sponge is now even bigger, ready to soak up new and interesting sights, sounds, and smells. Their awareness of the world is increasing, and this is an important time to begin exposing them to activities that will help them develop skills in all different areas. Research on brain-based learning in young children shows that their brains develop in spurts, the first occurring around the time they turn two. During this time, "the number of connections (synapses) between brain cells (neurons) doubles. Two-year-olds have twice as many synapses as adults. Because these connections between brain cells are where learning occurs, twice as many synapses enable the brain to learn faster than at any other time of life."[1] We come to understand from this that the things your toddler learns now can make a significant impact, even beyond this stage of development.

Being two is all about the three M's: mobility, memory, and me. These three areas all tend to overlap, but each one plays a significant role in what your child is experiencing during this stage of their life. If you pay special attention to how to help them learn and grow in these areas, you'll be able to better support them and will likely have a happier and more confident toddler.

MOBILITY

You may already have, or will soon have, a small and busy human running, tripping, crawling, and rolling across your floors. Every day can seem like an injury waiting to happen as your adventurous child looks for ways to move and explore without any parental help. You can probably tell that climbing on the back of the couch might end badly for your toddler, but there's also no reasoning with them on this. Two-year-olds are active and need to move around, receive sensory input, and test their limits in order to learn.

Stanford Children's Health says that although kids progress at different rates, most in this age group will have reached certain mobility milestones, like walking and running well, jumping awkwardly, standing momentarily on one foot, turning doorknobs and lids, flipping pages in a book, or drinking through a straw. They will also, according to Stanford, probably develop right- or left-handedness sometime during this year.[2]

With the development of gross motor skills and muscles and also fine motor skills during this stage, your child has probably also become a professional at play. According to Brooke Junior, MEd, a board-certified behavior analyst, kids between the ages of two to three can start to throw, kick, and catch balls; climb on playground structures; build towers with increasing numbers of blocks; and begin to ride a tricycle.[3] As your child moves and become more mobile through play, they also build better dexterity and grow stronger physically.

Research presented by Parenting for Brain highlights other key benefits of play, showing that, among other things, it stimulates brain development, improves intelligence, sparks creative thinking, improves communication skills, promotes impulse control and emotion regulation, helps grow social competence and empathy, contributes toward good mental health, strengthens relationships with others, and teaches life skills.[4] At the same time that your child is having fun, they're developing and their brain is responding; the physical, mental, and emotional benefits of play are contributing toward a healthier, happier, more confident kid.

MEMORY

By around the age of two, your child's mental and memory capacities have increased, and as with other areas of their growth, they are making significant gains. Toddlers are typically now able to sort items into categories, find objects hidden under multiple layers, complete sentences from books they're familiar with, play simple make-believe games, and follow two-step instructions.[5] Their ability to begin recalling memories is also developed during this time, as your child becomes more aware of who they are.

If you try to think back to when you were two, you probably have vague recollections of running around your childhood home, eating particular snacks, or playing a game with a parent. These may be distorted fragments of what we *think* happened around that time, but it's interesting to realize that colors, scents, feelings, or impressions from this age could have helped shape who we are today. For this to happen, research presented through Pennsylvania State University indicates that we needed to first develop a sense of self and personal identity, something that typically happens around one and a half to two years of age. "Having a sense of self, the 'I' separate from others, gives a place for memory to be organized and develop personal meaning," the research tells us.[6]

Without the realization of self, memory would be a much different tool for humanity. But because we are all unique individuals, given a sense of self and identity by God, our brains tend to keep track of things happening around us, and God uses what we learn and recall to bless us, grow us, and redeem us. Your child's ability to remember particular skills, truths, and details is part of their personal life journey. As parents, we can foster an environment that helps them understand what's happening, so they're better able to process and make sense of things. We can continuously provide them with love, assurance, safety, and a lens through which to view God through their circumstances, and in so doing, we offer our kids a positive, grace-filled way to comprehend life and their place in it. This guides them toward a healthy sense of self, a good understanding of how much God loves them, and the ability to feel confident.

Your child's memory is key to their ability to use their imagination too. God has given us imagination as another amazing tool to help us perceive the world around us. This is especially important for your two-year-old. With life still very new and likely confusing, their imagination can help them put things together in fun, understandable, and meaningful ways. Researchers have found that imagination also allows toddlers to improve their vocabulary, experience and practice a sense of control, learn societal rules, and problem solve.[7] I've seen it boost self-esteem as well, indicating that a healthy imagination can contribute toward a confident, well-adjusted child.

ME, ME, ME

As quickly as your child is growing, they're still a baby. You'll probably notice that most toddlers at this age have not yet developed the ability to give in, compromise, adapt, or share. They'll have big feelings, and they'll let you know about them. The fact that your child may be inflexible, rigid, or unreasonable isn't a character flaw but rather a reflection of what they're capable of at this stage. This is the "Me" stage of development; it's healthy and essential, but it will, at least for a little while, probably feel like the "Me, me, me" stage.

The "terrible twos" is a term that's often used to describe how two-year-olds behave when their bodies are going through a lot of developmental changes. You'll see wide fluctuations in their moods and behaviors, and you won't always be able to guess when these are coming. Toddlers in this stage seem to want and need us in one moment but then insist on pushing us away in the next. One second your child may be hugging your leg and, a second later, may start screaming and throwing toys for what appears to be no reason at all.

Many child experts cite the tremendous number of physical, intellectual, emotional, and social changes happening during this time as the basis for the terrible twos. Toddlers are able to understand a lot more from the inputs they've received, but they become frustrated when others don't immediately understand how they're expressing ideas or practicing new skills.

As well, according to the Mayo Clinic, "two-year-olds are struggling with their reliance on their parents and their desire for independence. They're eager to do things on their own, but they're beginning to discover that they're expected to follow certain rules. The difficulty of this normal development can lead to inappropriate behavior, frustration, out-of-control feelings and tantrums."[8] Your toddler must go through a normal process of self-realization, and this isn't easy for them. They can comprehend themselves and the world around them better than when they were infants, but they're still only just two years old and are experiencing what they're feeling for the first time.

Stanford Children's Health says that at this age, most toddlers will have a vocabulary of around fifty words. They'll be able to ask for common foods by name, make animal sounds, combine words, say "mine," and repeat words they hear from adults.[9] These are great milestones, but toddlers, still limited in how they can communicate overall, will find it frustrating when others misunderstand their meanings or intentions. Your child just wants to be able to express themselves to you; it seems simple in their eyes, so it's probably going to be upsetting to them when they can't get their message through.

The terrible twos are a normal phase of development, and there's no doubt kids around this age are going through a lot of changes related to self-realization, feelings of independence, and frustration from skills they're still working on mastering. This is a real phase. I will note, however, that we should also make sure to fully see our kids and how they're uniquely navigating through it. The way one child experiences growth and development during this time is not necessarily the way another will. Your toddler may experience some of these changes before or after other toddlers, and they may have feelings and responses that you can't just put a label on.

Some child-development experts believe that society exaggerates the terrible twos and how a parent reacts to their child's changes influences the extent to which this phase is actually "terrible." I encourage you to listen well to your child, be patient, gently help them through this stage, establish good patterns and habits that set them up for success, and extend a lot of grace to them (and yourself!). What you, your child, and your family will experience during the terrible twos is both a reality and a myth. There will be feelings and situations you can't prevent, but you have a say in how to make it better. Your child *will* come out on the other side of this stage of development and, with your help, will be more positive, well-equipped, and authentically confident than before.

Parenting, at any stage, can be overwhelming. When you have a two-year-old struggling through challenging developmental milestones, it's easy to feel worried or fearful if you aren't sure that what you're doing is working. All parents go through this, so don't be discouraged. We have so many resources available to us and wisdom and help from our shared experiences. Ask questions, seek information, and take your fears and worries to God, who is always faithful to act on your behalf. If you feel you're in the dark, John 8:12 reminds us that Jesus will light the way for whatever you need: "Again Jesus spoke to them, saying, 'I am the light of the world. Whoever follows me will not walk in darkness, but will have the light of life'" (ESV). With Christ, you'll be able to see your way through, feel more confident and peaceful, and learn how to love your child even better.

Having a two-year-old presents a whole new slate of challenges but also an opportunity to grow as a parent. God uses the difficulties in our life to grow us in grace, maturity, and understanding. Through this process of parenting our kids, He does a wonderful, redeeming work in us because He not only wants what's best for our kids but also what's best for us.

Confidence Building Blocks

Your child is moving, chatting, piecing ideas together, and testing the waters of independence more and more as each day passes. With all these essential developments, helping them build their confidence is vital. When we do this, we enable them to achieve a greater sense of self-worth, understand who they are in God, and feel like they can take on the world. Many child-behavioral specialists say that how a child views themselves affects what they do and how they do it. If we cultivate confidence in our toddlers, we can set them up for everyday successes, relational happiness, and good mental and emotional health.

So what are some of the practical steps we can take?

SHOW THEM WHAT PATIENCE LOOKS LIKE

When I was younger and a little more zealous, I'd pray grand prayers in my room during my times alone with the Lord. One of the requests I'd ask for most was to have more patience. I wanted patience to endure my surrounding situations and patience to learn from those around me. I quickly found that it was one thing to pray for patience but a whole other thing to just have it in my daily life. You see, I'd pray for patience, and then expect myself to become more naturally patient. The problem was that I didn't feel any different during difficult situations and, in fact, began to be *im*patient when my circumstances didn't change. Why didn't God remove the difficulties? Why didn't I suddenly just feel fine about them?

When I mentioned this to one of my mentors at the time, he laughed. He suggested that at these times, I open my eyes to see what God might be trying to teach me *through* the difficult situations. I wanted patience to be given to me, but God knew I would grow more as a person if I learned and practiced patience with His help. Similarly, in a scene from the movie *Evan Almighty*, God, played by Morgan Freeman, explains to actor Steve Carell's character that when we pray for patience, He does not always give us patience but instead the opportunity to *be* patient.[10] I believe that being calm and patient with our two-year-old provides us with just such an opportunity.

Patience is learned, and it's learned for our entire lifetime. There are no shortcuts, or we would miss out on the beauty, grace, and valuable life lessons we need to reflect God's glory and goodness. For us as parents, yes, we will struggle and feel frustration, resentment, anger, and pain, but patience is an amazing tool and character trait we and our children need. Your toddler might be the greatest teaching tool God will offer you in your life, and you, in turn, can begin to lay a solid foundation for a life of patience, peace, and authentic confidence for them.

One word you'll hear from your two-year-old a lot and probably early on is "no." It might be every other word out of their mouth, and they've probably spoken it as well as screamed it before a nap-time or while running from a bath. Toddlers seem to love the word "no" and all its associated power. While their feelings are valid, we can look for ways to teach more "yes" moments instead. Your toddler is only starting to understand the rules, and what you know is best for them may not be what they think is best for them. If your child rolled around in some dirt or sand outside, has pudding or spaghetti sauce all over their face, or gotten into some paint, they may not mind as much as you do (and might even be enjoying the reaction they're receiving). If they reject a change of clothes, wash-cloth, or bath, try understanding things from their point of view and softening your facial expression and tone, but also show them why cleaning up might be a good idea.

Showing your child patience and giving them time, even if you are exhausted, burnt out after a long day, or behind schedule, will show them that *they* matter more than other things. When you accept their emotions and model patience (this includes during a tantrum), you have created a teaching moment instead of a destructive one. Your child will see that even if you have a different opinion, you have cho-sen to be on the same side they're on rather than on the opposite side.

"To a toddler, leaving the park may feel like the end of the world. Help her get comfortable with her emotions by labeling them. Say, 'I understand you're sad because we have to leave the playground.'

By accepting her emotions without judgment, you validate her feelings and show that you value what she has to say," recommends BabyCenter, a leading parenting resource.[11] I've found that acknowledging feelings and demonstrating genuine care during a conflict not only preserves the relationship with your child in that moment but also potentially enables you to resolve the situation more positively and productively. You can both come out intact and feeling okay.

Teaching patience to your toddler also means that you allow them to make mistakes. If they accidentally break your favorite mug or drop food onto the brand-new carpet, help them understand what they could have tried differently to prevent the accident. Showing them what a cup can do when placed at the very edge of the table is more productive than snapping at them. If your negative emotions rule the situation and they are alarmed or upset, their synapses will fire negative messages and perpetuate the problem. Over time, they may learn to be afraid to make mistakes, and their confidence will suffer. But if you can be intentional about demonstrating kindness and patience, their synapses will fire positive messages that their brains will remember. Doing this facilitates learning and can also bring about a better outcome. Maybe next time, they'll know where to place that mug, and their reasons for doing this won't be based in fear but rather understanding. Happy, well-adjusted kids who feel we're on their side become confident kids who have a healthier view of grace.

If it's hard to find patience in a particular situation, I encourage you to think about what you're asking of your toddler and how difficult it actually is for them to do, especially given their limited perspective and lack of life experience. As grown-ups, we have plenty of things we don't want to do, and I venture to say that we probably throw our own age-appropriate tantrums more often than we'd like to admit. When we see a two-year-old throwing a tantrum, we should consider what we ourselves might look like to God when we're doing the same thing. Do we obey God perfectly every single second of every day? I sure don't, and I know I can behave just like a two-year-old to God, my Heavenly Father.

But God still expects obedience from us, just as we should from our children because we love them and need to teach them how to live. I can't help noticing that God doesn't lash out at me or throw me out of His sight every time I mess up or throw a tantrum. The Bible tells us that God is Love, and when I read 1 Corinthians 13 (ESV) and substitute the word "Love" with "God," I see a character description of God that reflects the way He's treated me again and again: "Love is patient and kind; love does not envy or boast; it is not arrogant or rude. It does not insist on its own way; it is not irritable or resentful; it does not rejoice at wrongdoing, but rejoices with the truth. Love bears all things, believes all things, hopes all things, endures all things. Love never ends." He is, among other things, patient, kind, loving, selfless, and understanding to me. He does this for my good, and he bears all things, no matter how I acted or what I thought I knew.

So when your child is struggling to do better and figure things out, remember that they, like us, need the same kind of love and patience we so freely receive all the time. Their attitudes might be challenging, but so are ours. I recognize that I'm a person in process who is in need of God's grace, and I would hate for Him to withhold His love from me when I'm not functioning at my best. Our kids would do well to receive this from us, and I believe it's our responsibility as parents to offer this to them. In what better way would they be able to grow, and in what better way can they learn about God and how He feels about them? I'd say that the terrible twos present us with countless golden opportunities to show them Jesus.

ENCOURAGE THEM

Encouragement is important to how a child grows. When we're intentional about providing encouragement and support during the twos, we help boost our child's self-esteem, validate their efforts, and make them feel more confident.

We can do this in all sorts of ways throughout the day by focusing on their strengths, providing them with opportunities to practice their talents, and showing them that we're listening to them. Encouragement looks like soft eye contact, a hug, a smile, or a nod. There are countless ways to acknowledge your child and to communicate that you love them and are proud of them.

Encouragement also looks like *not* doing certain things, like not responding harshly, not criticizing, and not comparing our child to someone else. We don't need to assume that we know exactly how our child feels, we don't need to talk over them, and we don't need to turn what might otherwise be a good teaching moment into something that's about us. Our toddlers, who are already grappling with a lot, should understand that grace is at the center of our relationship with them, our parenting choices, and the family dynamic.

The Child Mind Institute points out a fine line between encouragement and praise. "One rewards the person while the other rewards the task," it says. "Praise can make a child feel that they're only worthwhile if they do something flawlessly. Encouragement, on the other hand, acknowledges the effort."[12] Like in religion, we don't want to only focus on "works" and what we can *do* for God. By grace and grace alone, we are saved. We need to emulate Jesus when we encourage our children and make sure they understand that their ability to be loved isn't dependent on what they do. If they only receive our love after doing a task, they'll begin to feel like they need to *earn* love. But if they perceive that they somehow fell short or haven't done a good job, this creates a problem. They won't have an accurate view of their worth or lovability, and this could undermine their confidence in the long run.

I believe we need to commit to encouraging our toddler's efforts to help them fully blossom. When challenges present themselves, let's celebrate the process or journey they undertook rather than just the outcome. If we're too focused on the results, we can lose the lessons God reveals along the way or even miss the entire point. Some of the most beautiful and most worthwhile lessons in life come from the peaks and valleys around our efforts.

Encourage your toddler as often as you can during this stage of their life. When they are excited to show you what they're learning, provide feedback that shows you care. When they succeed at certain tasks or even just make an attempt, let them know you're proud of them. And when they exhibit signs of confidence, compliment them.

HELP THEM EXPAND THEIR HORIZONS

Because of the number of synapses your child has at this age, their brain can take in a huge amount of data. The experiences and stimuli they receive now are crucial. You are still one of the key influences in your child's life, and you can take this time to teach them more about all sorts of things.

Play, as mentioned earlier in the chapter, is an excellent way to help your toddler learn. If they are the ones to start or suggest the activity, it's even better because the game will hold their attention for longer and will probably be more fun for them. As your child engages in active play, they engage their neurons. They'll receive the benefits of healthy play, along with better self-esteem and a higher level of confidence.

You can introduce your child to new settings and situations too. To help them feel secure and set them up for confidence, you can tell them what to expect beforehand, so it's not a surprise. Allow them to mentally and emotionally prepare. If you're going to take them to a grocery store, for example, you can let them know it might be crowded, that you're only stopping in quickly to purchase three things, and that you'll go home afterward. You don't need to overprotect, but thinking about how a particular experience will go can increase the chance that it will be more enjoyable for them, which in turn leads to greater confidence.

At this young age, kids can already be given certain responsibilities. Simple age-appropriate chores can be a great confidence builder and help your toddler see what they're capable of. They'll likely be thrilled to be tasked with a chore and contribute to the family. "Beginning around age two, children can do small jobs around the house. To hold a child's interest, choose tasks the child has already shown an interest in," says one pediatric site.[13] Your toddler can match socks from the laundry basket, pick up toys, straighten sofa pillows, place napkins on the table, or pull the covers up on a bed, for example.

When introducing your child to new skills, break things down into small steps. You can also explain the whys, show how it's done, and allow for repetition, so they can approach things with more information and know that they have the opportunity to practice. Encourage them for their efforts, and adjust your explanations if you can tell they need it. Confidence will come if they feel okay in the situation and know that they'll be accepted, regardless of the outcome.

ESTABLISH HEALTHY PATTERNS AND HABITS

Your two-year-old is impressionable, so establishing healthy patterns and habits with them early on sets them up for smoother sailing later on. If you build a good foundation, your toddler will not only develop their best habits but also begin to understand why particular ways of doing things are beneficial. Whether they're eating, sleeping, learning, socializing, playing, accomplishing a task, or even just looking for something to do, they'll be able to rely on and find comfort in the habits and expectations around these that you're lovingly teaching them now.

The habits you set for your toddler will be specific to their needs and the rhythm of your family, and this may look different from what you see other families doing. Your toddler will probably come to recognize that basic habits, like brushing teeth twice a day, regular baths, responsible hand washing, practicing good manners, showing respect, or staying active, apply to every member of the family as well as to other kids outside the home. Some habits may be more unique to a family or change with the ongoing growth of the child; if a toddler likes to chew on their hair, repeat everything people say, hit when they're upset, draw on walls, or run away when they're called, you'll probably want to figure out how to address these behaviors and establish guidelines and habits around them.

Practicing and repeating good habits with your toddler will help them learn, allowing them to develop mastery with certain skills and establish patterns they'll remember. According to Montessori educators, "Learning requires electrical energy to create neural connections. . . . In adults, these neural connections are well developed based on previous experience, repetition and practice. . . . In children, these neural connections are only beginning to be formed."[14] Repetition, these educators and other child experts believe, is great for toddlers because it strengthens the connections in their brains, which is foundational to learning and memory.

Some of the habits will focus on specific areas. There will, for example, most likely be a set of rules and accepted behaviors around just mealtimes alone. You may need to help your two-year-old practice and repeat habits having to do with chewing with the mouth closed, holding utensils correctly, remembering to use a napkin, not bringing toys to the table, listening while others speak, not complaining about the food, eating nutritious food, reaching across others, or asking to be excused. Whatever the situation, if you help your toddler form good habits and are consistent in the way you reinforce them, you'll enable your child to retain knowledge that benefits them now and serves them well for a lifetime. The child who knows what's expected of them, feels safe in those expectations, and acquires the skills they need, can become a confident child.

A WORD ABOUT SCREEN TIME

I'd like to also add some observations around a habit that I've seen develop in my lifetime and one over which doctors, child psychologists, licensed therapists, and educators have expressed concern: too much screen time. It's an amazing technological boom we're in, exciting in so many regards. We now have smartphones, tablets, and computers that provide us with instant communication and the ability to traverse the Web, watch videos, play games, use apps, shop, take high-res photos, map the world, and connect with almost anyone. We have advanced gaming consoles and TVs with high-definition displays that capture our attention through virtual reality, augmented reality, facial recognition, voice recognition, gesture control, and incredible graphics. Some of the technology is even wearable. All this isn't necessarily a bad thing, but it shows that our world is drastically changing, just like your toddler.

I'm not that person standing on the corner with a picket sign demanding for kids to stop watching TV or playing with computers or tablets. I see a lot of good in the advancements that have taken place so far. But I note all this because technology is the new normal for the younger generations. According to the World Economic Forum, kids are going online younger and younger. They're commonly borrowing smartphones or tablets from their parents because they don't have their own, and even for the parents who share their digital devices with their kids for learning or other purposeful uses, "for children it's all about a fun way to fill the gaps in the day."[15] Should you allow screens for your toddler to engage them in learning or to occupy them when they're bored? If so, when? And how much is too much? All these are questions being asked these days, and it has added another element to parenting.

To me, the issue of screen time matters for your two-year-old because patterns and habits start now. Research is showing that this age is around the time most children will be introduced to technology in some way, shape, or form. For today's kids, technology will grow in influence over their world almost by the minute, and I believe everything your child sees and hears, especially over these next five years, will be stored in their subconscious mind for the rest of their life. These stored thoughts, impressions, and associated emotions become the filter through which they perceive the world, deal with problems, engage in relationships, and figure out where they fit in the big scheme of things—and neither you nor they will really know the extent of internalization.

The research on the long-term effects of screen time is still developing, but we've seen enough studies already that tell us too much screen time for children is not healthy. According to a large study cited by BBC News online health editor Michelle Roberts, "Letting a toddler spend lots of time using screens may delay their development of skills such as language and sociability."[16] The American Academy of Child and Adolescent Psychiatry has found that too much use can lead to sleep problems, less time with family and friends, not enough outdoor or physical activity, mood problems, weight problems, poor self-image or body image issues, fear of missing out, and less time to realize that there are other ways to relax and have fun.[17] The Mayo Clinic says it can be linked to behavioral problems, impaired academic performance, or a desensitization to violence.[18] And Reshma Naidoo, Director of Cognitive Neuroscience at Nicklaus Children's Hospital in Miami, says that "watching screens is passive and two-dimensional, both of which aren't good for developing brains." He observes that with too much screen time, children are exhibiting dysfunctional social patterns and are more responsive to media.[19] The research goes on and on.

I urge you, as a parent, to do your own research and see what makes the best sense for your child and family. We can't ignore the growth of technology, but we *can* be aware of it and form smart habits and patterns around it to help our kids learn to be wise, make good decisions, and become more confident about who they are. The American Association of Pediatrics recommends that children younger than eighteen months have zero screen time unless they are video-chatting, and kids between the ages of two and five be limited to screen use of one hour per day of parentally supervised high-quality programs.[20] It's best also to ensure that your toddler doesn't miss out on real face-to-face interactions, regular human touch, and opportunities to use using their senses; with these, they'll be able to build the strong brain connections they need to thrive.

Good habits will help our kids grow up healthy and happy. Age-appropriate online videos may not be the problem in and of themselves, but videos are more accessible than ever, so if we're not careful, too much exposure or the wrong kind of exposure may negatively affect your child's brain and self-esteem. We don't need to let online content raise our kids any more than we need to let Hollywood raise our kids through movies. We can provide our two-year-old with positive, encouraging, educational, and fun activities, both online and offline. We can be the parent that feeds our child what is good for their brain, and we ourselves can model good habits around screen time too.

Whatever we do, let's build habits that allow for genuine and lasting relationships and accurate views of who we are before God. Technology can be a great tool, but it shouldn't be a barrier between us and the relational bonds we're called to have with others or with God. With prayer and intentionality, I believe we can find a way to both limit and leverage digital devices so that we can enjoy the time we have with people, especially our child. They'll grow fast enough—the first eight years will fly by—and we have right now to love, teach, protect, inspire, and encourage our toddler toward a lifetime of authentic confidence, rooted in God's grace and goodness.

Raising your two-year-old is a full-time endeavor, and I understand that life doesn't necessarily give you the time, resources, or energy. To raise a confident child, I encourage you to apply the building blocks you've learned in this book so far, using them as a starting point, customizing them as needed, and then allowing God to inform what what's best for your child and family. Take care of yourself and your relationships with other family members too, so the dynamic in your home is a healthy, happy, God-honoring one. If you're married, nurture your relationship with your spouse.

The Bible says in Matthew 22:37–40 (ESV), "You shall love the Lord your God with all your heart and with all your soul and with all your mind. This is the great and first commandment. And a second is like it: You shall love your neighbor as yourself. On these two commandments depend all the Law and the Prophets." This verse tells us to love the Lord with everything we've got. Then we're called to love our neighbor—anyone that God has chosen to place around us—as much as we love ourselves. If we have a family, our "neighbors" include our spouse and kids.

The second commandment described here is interesting because it acknowledges that we should also have love for ourselves. I believe that how we love ourselves is often reflected in how capable we are of loving others; to me, this means we need to make sure to slow down to hear God and allow Him to remind us that we are His beloved. It's only in the overflowing, never-ending love of Jesus that we can truly begin to grasp how secure we are in His goodness and grace and then, in turn, have love to give.

I pray and hope that this year with your toddler is one full of goodness, grace, and love for you and your family. Cling onto the hem of Jesus's cloak every moment, remember the whys behind the actions of your little one that you learned in this book, and let Him guide you and your child to a place of authentic confidence.

PRAYER

Lord, today I make a commitment to reflect on your deep, unfailing love for me. Forgive me for the times I forget that you chose to make me in your image, that I have an identity in you, and that you pursue me every day with your love. I pray that you would change and correct my focus and perspective so that my love for you and others deepens in a way that brings you honor. Help me specially to love this wonderful child you have entrusted to me. Give me the strength and endurance, Lord, to raise the child you have called me to raise. I desire to be a great parent for them, and I need you to show me how to do that. In the name of the great I Am, amen.

Chapter 3

AGE THREE:
A LITTLE HUMAN WITH
BIG QUESTIONS

———⟨∞⟩———

Then children were brought to him that he might lay his
hands on them and pray. The disciples rebuked the people,
but Jesus said, "Let the little children come to me and
do not hinder them, for to such belongs the kingdom of
heaven." And he laid his hands on them and went away.

—Matthew 19:13–15 (ESV)

As much as we love our children, sometimes we need a reminder
that they are people too. Just because they can't yet communicate in the same way adults can doesn't mean they have less to
communicate. And just because their thoughts and ideas about the

world are still developing doesn't mean these should be overlooked. I believe it's never too early to value our children's words, observations, and sensibilities.

In Matthew 19, Jesus has gone to Judea, and large crowds of people follow him, hoping to have Him place His hands on them for healing or help. Word of what Jesus can do has spread, and Jewish leaders, there to test Him, want to debate and challenge Him. Some people bring their children to Him for His blessing, but the disciples step in, rebuking the people for wasting the Savior's time. Given the ongoing conversations with adults, this doesn't seem like a time or place for kids. I can imagine if I were there in that time period, I would probably be agreeing with the disciples.

As usual in His life and ministry, Jesus does things a bit differently than what we might expect. He says to let the children come. We see him welcome the children, lay His hands on them to bless them, and proclaim that the kingdom of heaven belongs to them. He teaches the disciples and all others who are watching that they are just as important as adults. He sees them as worthy of His time, love, and respect, regardless of their age, stature, or ability.

This, I really believe, is precisely how we need to emulate our responses to our children. Have we ever dismissed, discounted, or overlooked them in the busyness of a day or hustle of life? Are we really seeing them and listening to them, recognizing that they're made in God's image and valued as much at this age as you are at yours? Or course, if our kids are constantly interrupting when someone is speaking, we can patiently show them why that's not okay, but regular life lessons aside, do we invite our kids to contribute to conversations in their own way? And do we welcome their participation and choose to spend time with them? We can learn and be enriched by our kids, even when they're at their youngest.

For me, Jesus's example in Matthew 19 goes hand in hand with another telling moment in Luke 9:46–48 (ESV): "An argument arose among them as to which of them was the greatest. But Jesus, knowing the reasoning of their hearts, took a child and put him by his side and said to them, 'Whoever receives this child in my name receives me, and whoever receives me receives him who sent me. For he who is least among you all is the one who is great.'" In this passage, Jesus's disciples (who often, like us, seem to miss the point) are arguing about who is the best among them. I personally feel this is a silly argument to have in front of the Savior of the world, but look at what Jesus does: He brings a child to stand right next to him, demonstrating that they have a place beside him and are welcome to be at the right hand of God. Then, he states that whoever receives a child, does the same to the Savior. He lifts up, honors, and cares for children, knowing they're often thought of as unimportant. He calls *them* great and establishes that those who are considered the least or littlest have a place with Him and with His Father in heaven. I would say that in this, He also sends the message that He welcomes those who have an honest, childlike faith.

Both of these verses make me think of the three-year-old. Your child has a lot more to say and try on for size at this age, and they need you. They are, in many ways, your disciple, and just like how Jesus was the guide and teacher for his disciples, you get to be that for your child. All those "why" questions your toddler began asking last year were just a taste of what's to come when they are three. Their curiosity for the world and life is bursting at the seams, and as parents, you have the great responsibility to be their guide. What an honor!

This year may also be one of the more challenging years you'll have as parents. Some like to label it as having a "threenanger," a three-year-old who takes on some of the attitude of a stereotypical teenager. But don't fret; with a better understanding of what's going on in your child's brain and some methods to instill true confidence in your little one, you'll be able to navigate this next year more easily.

So, I say, let the children come. Lifelong patterns are developing now at this young age, and you can teach your three-year-old skills and truths that will bolster them well into their adulthood. Pour God's love and acceptance into their hearts as much as you can, let them be at your side, communicate to them that they're valued, and show them the deep meaning God provides in this life.

Three-Year-Old Brain Activity: The Age of Whys, Whats, and Hows

During the threes, your toddler's world (and therefore your world) revolves around the whys, whats, and hows. As I'm sure you expected, many new developments are happening within your growing toddler's brain because of that. This began in the previous year, but your child is now a little more aware of their surroundings, and they have more life experience. Words are coming easier, noises and smells are more recognizable, and they can concentrate for longer.

But one thing remains the same: A plethora of information is coming at your child, and they are trying to catch it all. Researchers have found that three-year-old brains "are more active and more flexible with more connections per brain cell, than the brains of adult human beings. . . . By the age of three, the child's brain is actually twice as active as an adult's."[1] We can easily forget how hard our little ones are working to learn and absorb. This can exhibit in recognizable ways in three-year-olds, including persistent questioning and negative reactions when they become overstimulated from learning new things; their reactions can take the form of fight-or-flight responses.

Their increased rate of learning will start to create positive behaviors; you'll see joyfulness in your child as they realize they can do something they couldn't before. At this age, family is everything to your little one, so you have the ability to help your child feel confident and secure as they seek to understand of the world around them, test new waters, and grow in their independence. This may not be an easy year for them, but with your guidance and encouragement, they will continue to do better.

QUESTIONS, QUESTIONS, AND MORE QUESTIONS

The world is a big and fascinating place, full of wonders that God created and called good. For your growing three-year-old, the magnificence of life and all its intricacies is new, mysterious, and exciting, and their sense of curiosity is emerging. *Why are clouds shaped like that? What's inside this pillow? How do hiccups happen? Where's that truck going? Can I go in the elevator? Why are you so tired?* Everything is interesting and something to be explored. That empty cardboard box in the hallway? It probably holds endless possibilities for them.

To begin with, your child is likely talking a lot more. According to Stanford Children's Health, kids this age can say between five hundred to nine hundred words, use speech that can be understood by others, speak in two- or three-word sentences and up to four- or five-word sentences, recall simple rhymes or lyrics, use "please" and "thank you," and refer to themselves by their own name.[2] It's probably exciting to see the advances your child has made with speech and also to know that you have a little human to chat with now. So long to the days of trying to interpret the unique and sometimes hilarious two-year-old language. Your child can now more effectively communicate about what they need and ask you any and all questions. *A lot* of questions. Get ready to try to keep up with all their verbalized thoughts!

What's happening in the brain that triggers their curiosity? Your three-year-old's brain is around 80 percent the size it will be when they are an adult, and within that space are a bunch of unconnected dots.[3] Your child, at this age, is trying to connect those dots to help make sense of the world around them. Your job as a parent isn't to have all the answers; no amount of reading or studying could possibly prepare you enough for this. But when they enter this stage of development, do expect to be interviewed daily by your child.

According to early education experts, it's likely that when your three-year-old asks questions, they may not actually be looking for answers. "Mostly they want to let you know that something you said and something they observed is interesting," says KinderCare. "When they ask why, it means they're curious and want to explore it further by talking about it with you."[4] I've found that you can support your kids' curiosity by engaging with them on specific topics, sharing what you *do* know, or asking them what they themselves might think an answer might be. *That's a good question. Why do* you *think babies need to take naps?* You can even search for answers together. If you can help your child build some problem-solving skills and encourage them to think for themselves, their self-esteem will develop, and they'll grow in confidence.

You'll find that your child asks new questions but can also repeat the same questions again and again. Even if the number of questions drives you a little crazy, know that this is a positive sign that points to their growth and development. It's also good that they are looking to you for acknowledgment and support. The worst thing we can do as parents is kill our child's curiosity or make them feel their questions are not worth asking. It is through their curiosity that they will begin to process truths about the world and who they are, uncover possibilities, and develop interests and hobbies that they may still have further down the road. It's our job (and our joy) to pay attention and direct their curiosity to help paint a clear, healthy, hope-filled picture of the world for them, nurture their sense of wonder, and allow them to become more confident, knowledgeable, and capable.

FIGHT OR FLIGHT

Around this age, as three-year-olds are busily learning and processing a lot, they can easily become overstimulated. This happens when they have more activities, experiences, or sensory input than they can handle in a given moment. In these moments, the alarm system in their brain overreacts to the situation. You might, at these times, see a neurological response that happens in kids and adults alike. It's call "fight or flight," which is an expression used to describe the

negative reactions we can have when we're overstimulated or trig-
gered. If you child experiences too much stress, feels threatened,
or is afraid—whether these sensibilities are real or imagined—this
can lead to the physiological reactions that make your child want to
either fight or flee. The higher the level of stress they feel, the stronger their fight-or-flight response.

A fight response might look like screaming, throwing, pushing,
kicking, or hitting. With this response, a child might hurl a toy
across the room if they can't figure out how to fix it, yell at a sibling
who isn't including them in an activity, or punch a ball when they
aren't allowed to go outside. A flight response might look like trying
to get away, fidgeting uncomfortably, behaving restlessly, or looking
around with darting eyes. With this response, a child might run in
the opposite direction if someone surprises them, back out of the
room if there are too many people around, or quickly turn away
when they hear a loud noise. You can sometimes tell a fight-or-flight
response is going on if your three-year-old seems grumpy or upset,
refuses to comply with things that aren't normally an issue, bursts
into tears, looks like they're tensing their muscles, or seems to be
breathing more heavily. These are all involuntary responses.

Remember that this is only their fourth year of existence, and with
all your child's questions and discoveries will come many moments
of frustration. "They don't know when a thing is harmless," says neuroscientist Dr. Dean Burnett. "They just know it's unfamiliar, which
can set them off."[5] And when they're set off, they may be unable
to listen to you or process your reasoning until they calm down. I
believe that if we're sensitive to the fact that our three-year-old is
prone to having these reactions, we can address situations in a way

that helps our child self-regulate and calm down, which will bring about a quicker resolution. Once our child feels better, we can guide them back to a place of security, happiness, and confidence.

So what do you do if you see that your child is having a hard time recovering from a fight-or-flight response on their own? Affirm them, encourage them to take some slow, deep breaths, and help them think through the situation calmly. Though their frustrating outbursts may push your buttons, make sure you're also aware of your own facial expression, tone, and body language. Your child will pick up on your cues, and you don't want to make the situation worse or draw it out for longer. Be patient, calm, and loving, allowing them to become less emotionally charged, so you can talk with them reasonably once again.

I recommend being preemptive about all this if you can. As a parent, anticipate when your child may encounter a frustrating or challenging task, is overly hungry or tired, is going to need to do something they don't want to do, finds themselves in a new or unfamiliar situation, or is about to transition from one activity to another. You might be able to help your child feel calm and secure before they even react. Fight-or-flight responses happen all the time, even to us. You don't have to step in every time if your child can work it out on their own. But when you're needed, be available to them.

Remember that your child's brain is developing faster at this age, and they're taking in a lot of input. Everything around your three-year-old is cause for question and observation, and their brain is constantly being stimulated and making millions of connections. Try to provide your child with good stimulation and varied activities, but keep watch and dial things back if you can tell they're reaching overstimulation.

Just give them a little quiet and assurance by letting them know you're there, and they'll be able to feel more secure and confident.

Confidence Building Blocks

Because your toddler is busy learning all about the world and themselves this year, their ability to develop and have a healthy sense of self is vital. You will need to take the time and effort to help build them up, show them they're loved no matter what, and teach them that they have a God-given identity. You'll, of course, do these things every year of their life, even beyond the first eight, but ensuring these are integrated into every part of parenting your three-year-old will help lay a solid foundation that can give them a strong sense of self-worth and authentic confidence.

So given this, what are some practical methods to instill confidence in your three-year-old?

TRUST GOD AS THE BEST SOURCE OF WISDOM

God is the best compass and source to turn to for help. We're made by Him, created in His image, and each designed uniquely. Unless we recognize we have an identity in Him, we will not fully know who we are or that we're not in the world by accident.

For your child to develop a sense of confidence, they'll need to understand that they're from God, He cherishes them, and there's nothing He wouldn't do for them. Conceptually, this can be difficult for a young child to grasp, but God created us so that certain truths resonate, even in those who don't yet know Him. As adults, we understand that this is where personal faith comes in, and one day, your child will hopefully reach that point in their life where they make a decision to follow Jesus. For now, in this fourth year of your child's life, you can go to God in prayer for wisdom on how to best raise your child, read His Word in the Bible, and seek to live a loving, obedient, God-honoring life. And as you do this, you can share your faith in everyday words and deeds with your child, model what it looks like to humbly and honestly follow Jesus, and extend grace to your child again and again in all situations, so they come to see and feel what God is about. The rest—the personal faith part— you can trust God to take care of. He's good like that, and no one knows your child better than He does.

You will have plenty of opportunities to discuss Jesus and the Bible with your child during this age. Because they are questioning all sorts of things at this stage of development, you may be surprised (and even amused) by some of the responses and questions they come up with, especially during prayer times or when you share parts of the Bible with them. I encourage you to be understanding and realistic about what your child can do at this age. They will likely not be able to sit still and take part in a Bible study as those older than them might be able to do, but you can share your favorite Bible stories with them or pick up a child-friendly Bible full of engaging pictures. When you read together, you can help them understand basic truths from the Bible, point out Jesus's qualities and characteristics, and connect these to situations in real life.

There are also many biblical stories or age-appropriate reading materials with a confidence-building theme. The story of Moses, for example, begins in the book of Exodus and shows the faith he needed to free his people from slavery. Because of his faith, he was able to have enough confidence in himself to confront Pharoah, the most powerful man in the world at that time, and approach him multiple times to ask the unthinkable. It's in stories like these that we can begin to paint a picture of what following God might look like and what's possible in life when we have a truly confident heart and mind.

I believe we should pray *for* our child and also *with* our child regularly. When they are part of a sincere and honest prayer life, they have the opportunity to see what it looks like to commune with God, ask Him for what we need, and especially, to express gratitude. Before bed is a great time to talk through a list of good things that happened during the day with your child and give thanks together to God for those things.

By instilling an attitude of gratitude at this young age, you can also help your child default to a heart of thankfulness. It will become a part of their subconscious to look for the good in life, something that not only shows God we appreciate Him but also has practical mental, emotional, physical, and social benefits that even science points out. According to Harvard Medical School, "In positive psychology research, gratitude is strongly and consistently associated with greater happiness. Gratitude helps people feel more positive emotions, relish good experiences, improve their health, deal with adversity, and build strong relationships." This research also shows that "people who are religious can use prayer to cultivate gratitude."[6] To count our blessings and give thanks to God is one of the best way to realize that in spite of the frustrations, disappointments, and hardships of life, He works all things for our good and His glory when we know and trust Him. He hears our prayers, even those we don't know to speak, and He shows us that in Him, the good outweighs the bad. In this, He also gives us the authentic confidence we need to live at our fullest potential. So when you cultivate your child's sense of gratitude, even at this young age, you bolster them for life and help them gain confidence.

As parents, my wife and I recognized that God gave us many tools for raising our kids that made all the difference. Among these are the ability to incorporate gratitude, love, and forgiveness in everything we do, allowing these to drive our parenting decisions. We sought to be grateful in all things, even the difficult moments, deeply love God and others, and forgive one another for our offenses, letting go feelings of resentments or unhappiness. These tools became our superpowers, and although we didn't do all this perfectly, we knew that our sons, our family, and each of us individually needed this to live confidently and at our best. Teach these to your little one, and I believe they will have an amazing capacity to deal with the challenges of life.

If you trust God with what He knows is good and right for your three-year-old, guiding them through this year of parenting can go more smoothly. It will be an adventure either way; God gives us great joy as parents but also uses the challenges of parenting to refine us and make us better as people. Don't be discouraged when all your best efforts and intentions don't seem to make a difference on some days. This is part of the process, and God will carry you through it.

LISTEN WELL TO THEM

I touched on the importance of listening to your child's thoughts and questions earlier but want to unpack this idea a little more here because at this age, it is so essential for them to feel validated and heard. Generally speaking, parents are used to having their kids listen to them, but kids who know they're listened to by a loving and engaged parent are more likely to be confident and resilient in life.

If you recall, research shows that the human brain can change. This ability, known as plasticity, allows our child to absorb what's happening around them, learn, and adapt to their environment. These early years are a critical period in which learning is easier for our young child, so they're amazing at taking in information.[7] When we demonstrate to them that they are worthy and what they say and think matters, this message is sent through countless neural connections, learned, and remembered. We are literally helping positively change our child's brains when they learn through us that they are cared about, understood, and respected.

As parents, we need to make a habit of listening to our kids and making sure we don't dismiss their thoughts or opinions just because they're young. We should listen without judgment, giving them time to gather their thoughts and words, and not feel the urge to correct. When we prioritize talking with our kids but giving them their own place in the conversation, we help them feel safe, acknowledged, and more confident; strengthen the bond we have with them; and gain more insight about what they're really thinking and how they're developing. We should make the conversations about them more often and ensure we're fully present, including putting down our digital devices.

When we do insert ourselves in the conversation, we should answer thoughtfully, speaking value back into them. We can use our experiences, including from own childhood, to help validate their feelings or struggles when it makes sense, as long as we bring the focus back to them. It can be a great thing to demonstrate honesty and vulnerability with our kids, establishing needed connections and drawing us closer to one another. This creates an accepting atmosphere in the family dynamic, and our kids will remember it even when they get older.

At the same time, keep yourself in check and make sure you don't accidentally take over the conversation when it's not about you. Try not to use your child as a sounding board for your own issues or problems. At this age, it's likely that they will simply not understand but instead absorb the negative emotions and feelings around them. Keep your interactions age-appropriate, and know the particular sensibilities of your child.

We have a lot to learn about our child when we listen to them. And I believe we have a lot to learn *from* them. Through the unfiltered responses and honest reactions of our three-year-old, we can be reminded not to limit ourselves, how to be curious and full of wonder, how to find joy in simple things, how to make the most of a moment, and how to say what we really feel. God gave us our particular child for a reason, so let's enjoy the gift that they are. Listen well to your child, learn from them, and engage with them thoughtfully and lovingly. You'll help build their self-esteem and develop their confidence, but I'll add that there's value in doing these things for everyone.

BUILD THEIR SENSE OF RESPONSIBILITY

Responsibility is the fertile soil where confidence can be grown. Think about life as an adult for a second. The responsibilities we take as parents, spouses, citizens, believers of Christ, employees, leaders, and more teach us profound lessons about life and build our character. How we accept and take on those responsibilities can build us up or tear us down and subsequently have an impact on others. I believe that as parents, we need to help our three-year-old develop a sense of personal responsibility that will allow them to begin to learn key life lessons, build their character, and set them up for later confidence and success in life.

Whether at school, at work, or in society, your child will eventually need to have certain skills and mindsets to contribute productively and to thrive. A three-year-old can learn now in an age-appropriate way that it's important to take care of things, think about others, plan ahead, solve problems, follow through, work through mistakes, and be trustworthy—among other lessons. One of the best ways to instill this in them is to start with simple household tasks and easy chores.

You may have already noticed this, but toddlers tend to love to be involved in the activities of a household, even helping out in any way they can. The world is exciting; there's a lot to learn, and they want to feel important and needed. Every day, they see us doing our daily tasks or following particular routines. We clean the kitchen, vacuum the floors, and do the laundry. We open closets, reach into drawers, and use fascinating tools and appliances. All the while, our little ones are often by our sides, observing what we're doing and likely asking questions. As with everything else, they are intrigued and likely want to explore some of this themselves. Given their interest, it's perfectly appropriate to build on the sense of responsibility you began to instill in your child at age two. The benefit this year is that your three-year-old is even more capable and has great capacity to understand.

Some parents worry that this is too young an age to allow their child to help out around the house, and I understand this. Three-year-olds are still, well, three years old. But I would argue that, as with two-year-olds, you can identify tasks or chores that won't be too much. If your child is following you around the house and seems to want some involvement, it's a very natural thing to include them, assuming they can safely handle the activity. Excluding them when they're asking about tasks or chores could also inadvertently send the message that they are not capable. Remember the sponge analogy from earlier in the book? Their brains can pick up on some of the unspoken things, subconsciously processing that we don't trust them or think they're capable of handling things.

Young kids love to do what adults do, and they enjoy feeling connected and important. Because they're motivated, you can easily build on these existing desires. At age three, they can attempt certain tasks around the house, like dusting, setting a table, carrying plates to a sink, cleaning up a spill they made, wiping a cabinet, putting away a game, returning books to a bookshelf, picking up after themselves, placing clothes in a hamper, making their bed, feeding a pet, or picking up leaves outside. When choosing tasks for your child, use common sense and don't push too hard if they don't understand what you want them to do.

Also, never criticize their work. It's very likely that your child won't be able to do the job as well as someone who's older would, but that's okay and not necessarily the point of assigning the responsibility. Go into this knowing that the chores or tasks your three-year-old handles might actually create more work for you, but the long-term benefits are worth it. If your child missed picking up a toy, for example, tell them gently or in a fun way that there's one more hiding in the corner. For them, cleaning up may simply mean picking up their blanket from the floor, and it may not have occurred to them to get everything else. Our job is to be patient, supportive, and understanding, slow to anger and quick to love. If you need to redo some of your child's work later on, don't let them see you do this because it could make them feel the job belongs to you and not them and also undermine their confidence.

At a primal level, allowing your kids to help you and take care of things builds the notion within themselves that they have what it takes to survive in this world. They need to feel a sense of purpose, recognize they're resilient, and know they're capable of accomplishing difficult tasks. They might not realize this directly, but internally and subconsciously, this is precisely what's happening. We want to instill in them a sense of responsibility so that they know a task doesn't belong to you but to them. To do this, we must teach them what we're asking, be explicit about what's expected, and then shower them with praise for what they've accomplished. As they work, reiterate your thankfulness and the importance of what they're doing. This will cause their confidence to skyrocket.

There's just something about three-year-olds that makes them the most wonderful helpers for mom or dad with the small things. Enjoy this timeframe, and make it fun. And know that getting them started now makes them that much more capable when they're older.

ENGAGE THEM IN ACTIVE PLAY

Another way to build your three-year-old's confidence is to continue to actively participate in their play. It allows you to connect with them and help them feel more loved and secure. According to the American Academy of Pediatrics, "As they master their world, play helps children develop new competencies that lead to enhanced confidence and the resiliency they will need to face future challenges."[8] Researchers have established that play is good for your child's development all around, including contributing to their healthy brain development, activating their imagination, helping them grow stronger, allowing them to engage more successfully in different situations and learn how to interact with people better. Play captures so many of the physical, mental, emotional, and social components that your child needs to be healthy, happy, and confident.

Though kids also require undirected play or play with other friends at times, I wanted to share in this section some simple tips and guidelines to support you when you do engage in play with your child. There really isn't a right or wrong way to do it, and you don't necessarily need a plan or specific toys. It can look like making stuffed animals talk or playing a board game, but it can also just as easily look like walking through some mud or lying on your stomach and studying the carpet together. "Let him be the 'director,'" advises Zero to Three, a nonprofit led by child-development experts, "Take on whatever role you're assigned, whether it is a T-Rex or princess, and have fun together. This lets your child know you value his ideas and see him as a leader, which builds self-confidence."[9] Participating in play with your child, no matter what shape it takes, allows you to enter into their world and tells them they matter, they are capable, and they are worthy.

When you give your child your undivided attention in play, you can also begin to get an idea of what they're feeling and thinking about. Three-year-olds tend to act out their emotions through imaginative play, so if we're watching them and picking up on their cues, we'll be able to have more of a finger on their emotional pulse. If your child is playing with a stuffed animal that is crying or sad, for example, this can be an excellent opportunity for you to observe them, ask some gentle questions, and help them work through a situation that at first seemed to be make-believe but actually ended up revealing real-life sadness or pain. If not for the time you had to play with them, your child may not have known how to articulate their feelings or find a good way to solve their problem.

Sometimes, it's not the play that's as important as the conversations and insights that come from it. As a parent, you can help pull back the curtain a bit to get at the heart and vulnerabilities of your child. You can pray and ask the Holy Spirit to minister to you and your child during emotional moments or ask God to create the opportunity to have the conversations your child most needs.

When my sons were much younger, we began a nighttime ritual before bed that I called "Three Questions." We built the time for this into our evening and after our nightly prayers, my sons knew they could ask me any three questions they wanted to. They liked Three Questions because it was a way for them to stay up later. I liked it because it gave insight into what they were thinking about at that moment. We wound up continuing this practice for over nine years, and the questions ranged from how light bulbs work to why kids were mean sometimes at school? I didn't always have the answers and sometimes, my sons and I would do some more figuring out the next day, but it was a treasured time that drew us closer and allowed us to think through life's questions together.

Whether you decide to try something like this with your three-year-old or not, it's important to remember that they're still very new to this world. You, as a parent, are currently their main source of information and main source of comfort. They need your guidance, perspective, and assurance to understand this giant and confusing place they find themselves in and know that they can face it.

We know that Jesus spent some time with children. I wonder how many questions he was asked. For that matter, I wonder how many questions the disciples asked him. We're all human beings looking to understand the world and our place in it. We all need God's comfort and the authentic confidence that comes from Him.

Your three-year-old is a blooming creation with many conflicting emotions and questions bubbling up within themselves. Be sensitive to the way they're taking in and receiving information at this age. Whether you are answering their questions, helping them through feelings of stress, playing with them, talking with them, helping them learn responsibility, or sharing about Jesus with them, keep in mind that they need your gentle, loving guidance to flourish and develop a sense of confidence.

PRAYER

Lord, no matter the situation, would you allow me to see all the good you've put in my day and my life? Help me to live a life of gratitude and stay focused on your positive impact, loving touch, and renewed grace every moment of my day. Even when parenting feels challenging or exhausting, show me how to be grateful for the amazing gift of my children and to be a good steward of all you've entrusted to me. I pray to be an awesome parent and to do the work necessary to improve daily. Lord, I ask that where I fall short, you take charge and draw my child closer to you, bringing them to a life of authentic confidence. In Jesus's name, amen.

Chapter 4

AGE FOUR:
PRESCHOOL ALREADY?

———————⦿———————

But when the chief priests and the scribes saw the wonderful
things that he did, and the children crying out in the temple,
"Hosanna to the Son of David!" they were indignant, and
they said to him, "Do you hear what these children are
saying?" And Jesus said to them, "Yes; have you never read,
'Out of the mouth of infants and nursing babies you have
prepared praise'?"

—Matthew 21:15–16 (ESV)

Not long after Jesus arrived in Jerusalem in Matthew 21, he
went to the temple. People who were blind or lame found
out he was there and went to him for help. The Bible tells us He
healed them, and children, who had seen His ability to do this,

praised Him with words that indicated they believed Him to be God, the Messiah. The chief priests and scribes didn't believe that Jesus was the Messiah and were furious about this blasphemy, but Jesus validated the children, giving them credit for what they had correctly understood. This didn't go over well with the chief priests and scribes because they didn't recognize Jesus's power and authority, and it makes me think of how children are sometimes so much more perceptive than adults.

There's something amazing about the pure, uncorrupted perceptions and sensibilities of a child. They see things for what they are, even if they don't always fully grasp what they're seeing. They don't worry about the same things adults do, they aren't burdened with people pleasing, and they're not socially conditioned to hold back their thoughts and opinions. The children in this passage of the Bible just knew who Jesus was and wanted to shout it out.

I love that the Bible reminds us that a child's faith is honest and powerful; it's adults who think they are already wise in their own eyes who miss the point. Let's pray that as parents we won't find ourselves the "indignant" ones in our child's story. We know we have much to offer our child, but we have much to learn from them as well.

My son taught me a lot when he was four years old. He was so unashamed of Jesus and His teachings that he would always ask me if he could pray to heal me if I was sick or hurt. What faith, I'd think, without necessarily expecting an improvement. But almost every time, my little one would pray a simple, honest, sincere prayer of healing, and I would feel better. There was no shouting out of verses, no exhuming of demons, no fog machine, no swinging of holy towels, or anything else we might see some televangelists do. It was a pure and simple faith that my little boy had, and it made me realize I needed to learn from the faith of a child.

In this stage of development, your four-year-old knows more than you may think. They are growing in independence, have more self-control, and can express themselves better emotionally. They're no longer quite as fragile as they were earlier on, and they're ready to build on their skills and continue branching out. Their world can widen during this stage—and they'll want it to widen.

This year is when some children begin preschool. If you observe that your child can focus on small tasks and finish them without a lot of redirection from a parent, can follow basic directions, can function well within a routine, shows interest in interacting with other kids, and is potty-trained, your child may be ready to expand their horizons in preschool. There, they'll have an opportunity to learn some academic skills and develop their social and emotional skills in a different context.

This doesn't mean that all children need to go to preschool to properly develop; I recognize that families have different ways of teaching their kids, including homeschooling, small-group co-ops, and distance learning. Regardless, your child will soon be ready for more, whatever shape that takes. You can have real fun teaching and playing with them in this year because they're simply capable of more.

Four-Year-Old Brain Activity: Change Is Good

Your child has continued to change immensely. According to neuropsychologists and professors Timothy Brown and Terry Jernigan, brain development during the preschool years "is characterized by its 'blossoming' nature, showing some of its most dynamic and elaborative anatomical and physiological changes."[1] Your four-year-old's brain is still rapidly growing, and they are absorbing even more. As it does, your child is bursting with new emotions, curiosity, and creativity. They are also experiencing new mental demands.

The Child Mind Institute says that, developmentally, four-year-olds can usually now tell stories, will have mastered some basic rules of grammar, can understand the difference between "same" and "different," will have a clearer sense of time, can follow three-part commands, and can understand the concept of counting, among other milestones. Your child can likely also negotiate solutions to problems and view themselves as a whole person with mind, body, and feelings this year.[2] According to parenting website Raising Children Network, preschool-aged children understand more about opposites like high versus low, know the names of letters, can sometimes remember their own address, and might know the difference between left and right.[3]

In terms of fine and gross motor skills, you'll probably see that your four-year-old is more dexterous, is stronger, and has more agility. They should be able to manage utensils during mealtimes pretty well at this point and also hold a pencil, use scissors, play cards, pour beverages, and dress themselves without help. You may also notice that they can catch a ball even better, stand on one foot for longer, jump higher, and walk backwards.

Your child is able to do a lot, which is something to be celebrated. They're preparing to move into the next stage of development and along with that, many will find themselves building on their skills this year in a preschool environment. Their world and their understanding of their place in it will expand, and you'll soon be helping them navigate the changes. They'll meet teachers, interact with other kids, learn new rules and expectations, follow different routines, sing songs they haven't heard before, play in different spaces, and discover new things. Their brains will take it all in and process it, and they'll need you to make them feel safe, guide them, and help them make connections.

Change is good for the four-year-old, whether the developmental changes and advances they're experiencing or the external changes they'll soon encounter in preschool. This year is one in which your little one suddenly doesn't seem so little anymore, and their brains are ready for more input, stimulation, and growth. Helping your young child make the transition to exciting new things this year will develop in them the confidence they need to do well.

Confidence Building Blocks

Authentic confidence becomes even more critical as your child begins schooling. We know that this era opens them up to so many experiences, including new friends, big lessons, and opportunities to grow as a human. This also exposes them to new challenges that can be stressful or frustrating. I believe that how we teach them to respond to all these experiences matters.

To help your four-year-old gain confidence before they start preschool and have a successful experience after they arrive, we once again need to turn to God for wisdom and direction. You began to lay a foundation of faith for your child in their first few years that you can build on now. If they feel that God is holding them steady and you are too, they'll feel more ready to face the unknown. At the same time, you can set their expectations for the different experiences at school, so they can go into it feeling more confident. Later on, both at home and at school, applying the strategies I touch on in this section will help them develop in independence and grow in resilience.

BUILD THEIR FAITH

As I mentioned with my four-year-old son earlier, kids are never too young for Jesus and His mighty ways. My son was so in tune with the Spirit of God and bold in his faith at that age that He believed God would heal me when I wasn't feeling well. I know that those who don't believe in God may find this to be pretty out there, but I'd say that just because a human being is younger and still learning doesn't mean they can't see certain truths. I also don't think that just because someone is a child, those truths are negated. God *is* good. God *does* have the power to heal. God doesn't want to see people in pain. He's honored when we, no matter how old we are, look to Him for help. And God answers prayers.

Some child development specialists note that spiritual thoughts and feelings are important to a young child's emotional growth. David Elkind, professor emeritus of child development at Tufts University, says that some kids "seem to be more openly engaged by the concept of a higher power."[4] It's healthy for a child to be able to ask questions about God and explore what it means to have faith, even if their observations seem simplistic to adults. The fact that they are looking to understand spirituality, along with everything else they're learning, is normal and I would say just as crucial as their mental, physical, and emotional development.

In this stage of life, your four-year-old is more of a literal thinker. They'll take things at face value and call out situations as they see them. Though there are abstract parts of following Jesus and understanding faith that are hard for a child this age to grasp, they're ready to learn even more about the heart and love of God.

Our job is to continue to teach them, demonstrate to them, and build their confidence in the ways of Christ. Even things that seem abstract for them, like trusting God and loving Jesus, can be modeled through our prayers, acts of kindness and care, personal sacrifices, and peace during difficult moments. Proverbs 22:6 (ESV) says, "Train up a child in the way he should go; even when he is old, he will not depart from it." If we show our child what Jesus is about when they're young, we lovingly equip them with the information they need to make a decision about their personal faith at the right time. I hope that when they're older, they'll be able to lean on the things we shared with them when they were children and find comfort in them.

At the same time that we're responsible for bringing God's truth and love to our child's heart and mind, I believe we also need to remember that they're growing to be their own person. We need to nourish them, just as God nourishes us, but He doesn't control us or force us to have faith. He didn't design us to be robots that can only do His bidding. Instead, He gave us free will, brains, different personalities, and unique tastes. He knows that real love and a life of hope and faith come when we choose Him, not when we are forced. To me, that's the best part about His kingdom. And this is exactly what we need to keep in mind as we guide and lead our child toward a life of faith; we can show them and teach them, but for them to truly follow Jesus, they have to believe Him and choose Him themselves so that their faith is their own and not just ours.

Trust God to work in your child's life. When we give Him room to move in our lives and our children's lives, special things can happen. And listen to your child's thoughts, concerns, or questions about God, Bible stories, and a faith-filled life. Openly walk in faith together with your child, and allow God to continue to mold your little one the way He knows is best. Your child's faith can deepen because of you, but it is not dependent on you.

As well, keep in mind that just being the adult doesn't mean you always have the better answers. God will most definitely use your little one to teach you more about yourself and His character. Your child is a gift and a blessing to you, and God gave you to each other because He knows that you both have what it takes to help make the other person who they were always meant to be.

SET THEIR EXPECTATIONS FOR SCHOOL

Your child may feel fearful or anxious at the thought of starting preschool. Their whole world up until now has been with you and at home, where the environment is safe and familiar to them. They know how to function well there but may have little concept of what preschool entails. Preschool is one of the biggest changes your four-year-old will go through this year, and they'll need you to help them feel capable, safe, and steady as they step out into the world a little more.

I'd say that as much of a change this phase of life will be for your child, it might feel like a bigger change for you as a parent. Sending a child to preschool for the first time, even if it's only for a couple of hours a day and a few days a week, means you recognize that your child is ready to grow in independence a little more. You are entrusting them to other authority figures and influences. You've hopefully selected a great preschool you're excited about and are looking forward to having your child learn from skilled teachers and make nice new friends. And even if you're looking forward to having more of your own time to work, manage household activities, or engage in other endeavors, preschool is usually the first time that parents are away from their child for a longer period of time. Don't be surprised if it takes some adjusting for both of you. Your child may naturally experience some separation anxiety when they start to attend preschool, and I'd venture to say that you might too. Unless you work and your child already attended daycare in prior years or your plan is to teach your child at home or through a smaller co-op, preschool is unfamiliar terrain, and reassurance will be needed all around.

One of the best things you can do to set your child up for preschool success is to prepare them. Begin to establish predictable routines at home and start talking about exciting things kids do in preschool. You can probably arrange for an early visit with the school, so they can see it. When you go, walk hand in hand with your child, let them meet their teachers, and point out artwork, craft supplies, toys, and interesting play spaces while you're there. Anxiety for both you and your child will be eased by introducing the change gradually and not thrusting them straight into the fire.

If your child comes to know what to expect, they'll feel more ready. It's sometimes fear of the unfamiliar that keeps people from being able to embrace change, but you can equip your four-year-old with helpful information and offer them perspective so that they might feel more confident. Your child has been by your side so far in life, and you have been their safe place to go for love and comfort. They trust you, and going to school doesn't need to change that.

You can let them know that you're still just as there for them as you have always been. Tell them you're so proud of them for how much they've learned and grown and that you are excited for the new experiences they'll have at preschool. Share with them what you've learned about the activities there and the structure of the day. Let them hear about their teacher. And tell them you'll be right there to pick them up when it's done and can't wait to hear all about it. Keeping things positive in tone will communicate to your child that preschool is a good thing and you're comfortable with having them go. If they sense that, they'll feel safer, braver, and hopefully even more excited about it.

I recommend being careful not to project your own worries onto your child. At this point in life, your four-year-old may not yet have any frame of reference with school. They may not actually be quite as worried or anxious as you are because they don't know the particular nuances of being there, learning new things, interacting with different personality types, or making friends. Instead of focusing on concerns that may not materialize into anything, you can trust that God goes before them into their preschool experience and will be there with them every day. He will guide their learning and their influences, and He will engineer the circumstances for their good and His glory because He loves them. So let your child experience it, free of any additional weight, and know that they won't be alone. Tell your child what you think their preschool day will look like and provide a positive outlook and perspective. Give them a chance to try it, do some figuring out, and come out on the other side more capable and confident. Knowing that your child will feel okay will, in turn, make you feel more confident and okay about them being there.

Keep in mind that the adjustment period is different for every child. They may need a few days, few weeks, few months, or even no time at all to make a comfortable transition to this new stage of life. Susan A. Miller, Professor Emerita of Early Childhood Education at Kutztown University of Pennsylvania, says that a child's temperament, needs, interests, and prior experiences all affect how a child copes with preschool changes. "Don't be surprised if some seem to revert to the familiar, less-mature behaviors of younger children (baby talk, clinging). In this way, a child may be telling Mom or Dad to stay a little longer at drop-off time," she notes.[5] Try to understand the aspects of the preschool day that your child is worried about. Be patient, comfort them, come up with some strategies that might help lessen their concerns, let them know they're capable, and fine tune the approach until they feel better. If your child takes longer than you expected to adjust, this doesn't necessarily mean you've made a mistake in sending them. Human beings grow, gain confidence, and become more resilient by doing hard things. After a while, those things may not be quite as hard.

During this time, you can share your own past experiences with your child, letting them know how you have dealt with worry or fear. Remind them that God is right by their side, and it's okay for them to talk to Him if they are afraid. Read to them some psalms or other verses that you've turned to in your own times of anxiety. Stories of faith like the one of David facing Goliath can be great because at this point in their life, preschool might be their own personal Goliath. You can talk about how David overcame his fear and put his trust and heart in God to defeat the feared giant.

I know it can be difficult for a parent to leave the school at drop-off if they see that their kid is crying out for them. Practicing independence and suddenly not having a parent right there by their side is a hard thing to ask of a child and is part of the process at this age. My advice is to give it time while being sensitive, loving, and supportive. Again, highlight the positives of the day and see if you can redirect their focus to an activity they may enjoy. Your child's teacher may be able to help with this as well. Once your four-year-old adjusts and becomes more comfortable with their new surroundings, going to school will be part of their normal routine, and they may even love and look forward to it.

Preschool is enriching and can also be a lot of fun for your child. It will allow them to build relationships, feed their brains, and engage their imaginations. Enjoy the stories they tell you about their day and watching their eyes light up with all they've learned.

ENCOURAGE THEIR INDEPENDENCE

Your four-year-old likely wants to handle more and more without your help. Their sense of independence is becoming more prominent to them at this age, and it's healthy to encourage them to try things by themselves. Independence promotes their self-esteem, makes your child feel important, and helps them become more confident. It also allows them to develop more of an awareness of themselves, become better decision makers, and gives them a sense of control over their life.

I encourage you to practice letting go of some of the control you were able to have in your child's earlier years. You won't be at preschool every day with your child to help them get along with all the other kids or ensure they understand what the teacher is saying. Instead, allow your child to face their challenges and take these on to the best of their ability. You can make wise suggestions and provide a framework for them to handle the challenges, but they'll never learn the important lessons if we continuously get in the way. If you hover too much, you could accidentally undermine your child's confidence. Make your child feel secure, and whatever happens, good or bad, reinforce the fact that you care for them and believe they can do it.

Beginning to develop your child's sense of independence can happen before they even begin preschool. For the four-year-old, playtime continues to be central to exploring their world, using their imaginations, boosting their creativity, thinking through difficult concepts, and gaining in independence. I mentioned many of the benefits of play in earlier chapters, but at this age, independent play is important too. It can help your child develop their sense of focus, problem solve on their own, learn more about cause and effect, and become more capable. If the tower of blocks fall, they can try again or redesign it. If a game piece doesn't fit, they can figure out how to angle it differently. If they are missing a toy, they can adjust their plan.

To encourage independence through play, you'll want to decide on how much time you want them to play on their own and then create a safe place for them to do this. Try to keep your eye on them, but don't necessarily be a presence in the room. This is their opportunity to explore, try, think, and do without feeling they'll be interrupted, corrected, or managed. The idea is to provide a structure that allows your four-year-old to direct their own play. When they do, they'll be more inclined to try things by themselves rather than just quickly ask you for help, which builds their independence and confidence.

With independent play, start out small—at first. If this is something your four-year-old hasn't yet done a lot of, they may not have the emotional stamina they need to do it. Let them feel free to explore the possibilities and assure them that you're nearby if they need you. They don't have to be able to play for thirty minutes by themselves; just enjoying five minutes of independent play can do the trick. If they're the ones driving it, they'll reap the benefits.

As well, some therapists recommend offering your child toys for independent play that they can engage with in many different ways. Certain electronic toys guide a child to interact in more focused and narrow ways, but if you give your child boxes, blocks, stuffed animals, cars, dress-up clothes, or other props, they can use their imaginations with these in any way they want. Children who feel comfortable playing on their own will recognize they're capable, which will help them feel more capable with different tasks and skills in other parts of their life.

There are many other ways to encourage independence in your child too. Simply allowing them to make choices, like what to wear or what to eat, can help them feel empowered. In many cases, you may need to guide them, providing a small set of age-appropriate options they can choose from. And when they make wise choices, you can praise them. They'll recognize that they are capable, that their opinion matters, and that there are ripple effects that go with their decisions. Giving your child the freedom to make choices about things fosters a deep trust between you and your child. If they believe that you trust their ability to make decisions, they'll gain confidence.

But at the other end of the spectrum, if we don't give our four-year-old opportunities to make choices or if we dismiss their ideas, they may come to believe that they're incapable or what they think isn't important. Kids need to be able to explore choices in a safe, healthy way. This is good for their self-confidence, allows them to grow at their best, and will also help them know that they are capable of making smart choices when they're older.

To help your child become more independent, you can give them the opportunity to solve problems as well. If they do something incorrectly, like buttoning a shirt wrong, give them the chance to correct it before you swoop in. Your reactions can affect them and how they view themselves. Simply observe the situation, and your child may figure it out after a while. Praise them if they do. If they don't, keep it positive and still allow your child to correct the mistake themselves. Learning from our mistakes can often be more important than the actual fix.

You can also have your child help out around the house in ways they haven't before. They can mix cake batter while you're baking, press the start button on the dryer, or find the bucket in the broom closet. This helps them feel capable and also allows them to build on skills they'll need to be more independent.

After your child starts preschool and is more acclimated, there will be all sorts of opportunities for you to help instill authentic confidence in them. When they come home with a picture or creation they made during the day, display it for all to see in the house. Celebrate the stories you hear from their teacher about their day; sharing a book, learning a song, comforting a friend, showing consideration to others, putting away bins, or following directions are all signs that your four-year-old is doing great at school, becoming more responsible, and figuring out their new world. You can also have your child help pack their own lunch for school. Can you imagine how good it will taste to them the first time they eat it? Regardless of how you choose to encourage independence in your child, enjoy watching them grow and become even more of their own person this year.

Your four-year-old will be experiencing a world of change. With the right understanding and support, they'll be able to face anything. Grow with them, learn together, lean on Jesus, and watch in awe as God leads you and your family during this amazing year of your child's life.

PRAYER

Lord, give me your wisdom as I become intentional about my walk with you and the importance of that walk for my child. Please give my child positive experiences at home and through preschool that help create the mind of a confident child of God and a happy, healthy human being. I pray that you would fill them more with your amazing and powerful love this year. Thank you that you know their every thought and are with them even when I can't be. And thank you that you are good and know the best way to raise my child. In Jesus's name, amen.

Chapter 5

AGE FIVE:
THE IN-BETWEEN

⌀

Trust in the Lord with all your heart, and do not lean on
your own understanding. In all your ways acknowledge him,
and he will make straight your paths.

—Proverbs 3:5–6 (ESV)

Age five is the confusing but exciting phase when a child takes
the first step toward the "big kid" years. They find themselves
somewhere between toddlerhood and an older sense of self. They
like the comfortable, familiar dynamic of their younger years and
yet they're excited by their growing independence. This age is full of
complex developments and contradictions, and you may find that
you're headed into some uncharted waters with your five-year-old.

At this point, you have several years of parenting under your belt
and have learned a thing or two about raising your child. Your child

has also come a long way and formulated some of their own thinking about who they are. It's easy now to begin to default to patterns of behavior we're used to or rely on our own strength in our everyday situations. But Proverbs 3 reminds us to trust God rather than leaning into our own understanding. If we don't realize that we're starting to go our own way, we could veer off the path or run into troubles.

I've found that the older I get, the more I think I know. While this is technically true, I can accept that I don't know more than God about everything. His understanding of the world, His creation, our hearts, our minds, and our children go beyond what I can ever comprehend. So trusting and leaning into God, I've learned, means that I need to relinquish my control over things, including what I think I know about my kids or parenting. I can choose to give God control of the circumstances of my life because I believe He knows best. Notice that Proverbs 3 says when we trust Him, *He* will make our paths straight. *He* will bring us clarity, and with *His* clarity, we have a way forward and can avoid getting lost.

Parenting isn't easy, and we need God's direction. I think also of Proverbs 16:9 (ESV), which tells us, "The heart of man plans his way, but the Lord establishes his steps." I'm grateful that as we make our way along the path of parenthood, God knows exactly how to direct our steps. My prayer is that as your child enters the fives, you would lean into Him whenever you're struggling and allow Him to take you step by step.

In much the same way, your child may be looking to you to know how to step into this stage of development. They need your direction and guidance and know they can trust you. Their world, as exciting as it can be, is continuing to change and though they may have ideas about what's best for themselves, they're also leaning into you, their parent.

My dad taught me to swim by introducing me to the water and holding on to me as I practiced. He knew I was safe because he was there to watch and hold me. But like many children who are new to the water, I worried that it was too deep for me, that it would get in my eyes, that I would sink, and that my dad would somehow not be able to get me. He showed me he was there and kept encouraging me until one day, I felt brave enough to trust him and jump in.

This is what your five-year-old needs from you this year. They're entering the water. It's fun but also scary and unfamiliar. They see that you're there with them, but they're not ready to jump in. They know you haven't let them down in the past, so they may do some trial jumps at some point. Each time you catch them in your arms and encourage them, they realize they can do it and become a little more confident. Eventually, your child will be able to enter the water and begin to swim more independently. They'll see you not too far away. The next time they meet a challenge, they'll look to you, leaning into you, and feel braver about stepping out.

Your role this year is to help your child recognize they can trust you and God in all the changes they have ahead of them. You have the privilege of ushering them into an older age and bringing stability, wisdom, and an understanding of God to their lives.

Five-Year-Old Brain Activity: Toddler or Big Kid?

Because ninety percent of brain growth happens before kindergarten, your five-year-old is still learning, absorbing, and processing at an amazing rate.[1] But now, their ability to acquire knowledge and comprehend the information is even more advanced. Neuroscientists note this advanced brain development in five-year-olds, including research that shows "The kindergarten brain . . . features many mental upgrades from a preschooler's: superior memory, beefed-up attention span, a tighter grip on reality, improved self-control and social skills, and a firmer grasp of knowledge codes—i.e., numbers and the alphabet."[2]

Your child's brain, like a beehive, is full of new activity, with thoughts and information buzzing like trillions of bees between synapses. Because they're mentally able to do so much more, they also feel pretty grown up. With the developments in their cerebral cortex at this age, your child will be way more attentive than they were even in just the past year. Not only that, but they will also be able to better retain information they hear, meaning they'll be able to sit still and listen to their teachers at school, as well as focus on your words at home. You'll find that your own discussions with them will be noticeably more mature.

You'll notice at the same time that these mature conversations will be mixed in with toddler-like meltdowns too. As mentioned, your five-year-old is on the cusp of the "big kid" era while still being a toddler at heart. This year for them will likely be a roller coaster of emotions and contradictions.

They've reached the kindergarten age and developed enough that they actually have more of an understanding of the changes and growth they're experiencing, and they'll now be able to better verbalize some of these changes to you. But the flashes of newfound maturity you see in them could also suddenly be followed with three-to-four-year-old behaviors. If your child doesn't want to eat their broccoli at dinnertime, for example, they can now articulate to you why they don't want their vegetables. But on another day, screaming "no!" about it might feel better to them. Age five has many old patterns of behavior, and more and more, these will give way to new patterns over time.

Surprisingly, you'll continue to see big growth this year with their emotions. They'll have moments of regression but also demonstrate amazing emotional maturity. I've seen that as adults, we can easily lose focus on God's command to love our neighbors. We may avoid interacting with people who disagree with us. We may be ultra-focused on our own way of doing things. We may forget we need to reach out to others for help. Or we may just be caught up in our own busyness. Five-year-olds, I've observed, can be filled with compassion and empathy for others. They notice those who are unnoticed and take God's command to love others at face value.

Children at this age have a natural ability to overlook people's faults. They are unfiltered and can be incredibly moody, but they accept you for who you are. I believe there's a reason Jesus uses children as an example of how we're supposed to act and see the world around us. Their hearts and minds, even at age five, seem uncorrupted by the world, and I wish I knew how to capture and hold the innocence and bold faith they seem to so naturally exhibit. Let's pray that we continue to lead them in Jesus and encourage their faith the best way we can, hoping they never lose that.

As our five-year-olds develop mentally, emotionally, spiritually, physically, and socially, what are some tools we can use to help them feel confident and protect all the wonderful qualities God gave them?

Confidence Building Blocks

It's possible, even in the "in-between" stage of development, for our child to be able to grow in authentic confidence. As they branch out and try new things, we need to give them opportunities to rise up and succeed. I believe that we should praise them when they confront challenges, that we should help them understand they are loved and accepted just the way they are, and that even when things don't work out, God has already offered His grace to them and a new beginning. They should know that failing is expected in this life and it doesn't affect their value as a human being or as our child. If we can encourage them as they navigate their way through this year and do our best to love them unconditionally, their confidence and sense of self can flourish.

PRAISE THEM IN A WAY THAT RESONATES

Honest praise is vital to the healthy development of a five-year-old. Many child development experts discuss the positive effects of praise, noting that it makes kids feel more motivated, inspires them to try harder, helps them believe that they can complete tasks, and elevates their sense of self-worth. Being praised for their efforts and hard work makes kids feel good.

But we also need to think about the *kind* of praise we give as parents. Some studies indicate that the wrong kind of praise may negatively affect a child or harm their self-esteem.[3] Parenting Researcher Gwen Dewar offers some evidence-based tips for praising kids better, including ensuring our praise is sincere and appropriate to the accomplishment, praising our kids for the things they can control rather than their innate abilities, and supporting our kids all the time, not just after they've accomplished something praiseworthy.[4] We want our kids to know we mean it when we tell them how highly we think of them and make sure we don't mistakenly cause them to feel bad when our desire is to bolster them. It's crucial too that they understand that our love for them is never contingent on their performance. If they tried something and didn't get the results they wanted, they should know that they can try again and we're there to applaud them for that too.

I believe it's important to praise our kids for what matters in the long run. They should know that we care about helping them cultivate positive character traits that honor God. Kindness, strength, patience, perseverance, hard work, selflessness, tolerance, and love are all examples of this. These are admirable qualities but can also be put into action and lived out in a way that blesses people and honors God.

Parents should also be careful to minimize the focus on a child's outward appearance, something that's especially important with girls. While we don't we need to ignore their appearance entirely, the way someone looks or dresses has no bearing on their worth or how lovable or capable they are. Imagine hundreds of billions of synaptic nerves dedicated to your self-worth that are somehow based on your physical appearance rather than the complex, many-layered parts of you that are capable of doing so much in the world. Good looks and physical beauty don't last, but our actions and accomplishments for God can leave a legacy. Praise your child and help focus them on the things that matter. Authentic confidence comes from this.

AVOID COMPARING THEM TO OTHERS

On this side of heaven, we often think about ourselves in relation to others, and it can be hard not to wind up comparing ourselves to them. When we do it with our kids, however, we risk making them feel anxious about possibly not measuring up. Even if the comparison is positive, the focus is on performance and not on what makes a person special and unique in the sight of God.

God gave us all different strengths, talents, and abilities, and no one has these in exactly the way that we do. He created us in the way He did for a purpose and a plan, and He delights in us just the way we are. But when a child is compared to someone else, the two are measured in terms of each other, rather than the way God might see them. It takes away from who they are.

The problem is that there's always someone who's smarter, taller, nicer, funnier, more athletic, better behaved, or more talented. How does someone ever *not* compare themselves to others? A child can easily always feel inferior or less than when compared to someone out there, which affects their confidence and self-esteem. They may also develop some social anxiety if they begin to perceive others don't think highly of them either.

At this age, your child still very much wants to please you and cares about your good opinion of them. Being compared to another child or a sibling can hurt their feelings, rob them of confidence, and be difficult to heal from. Their worry that they may disappoint you could also cause a strain on your relationship with them. The bond you share is important, and you don't want your child to withdraw or hide how they're really feeling from you.

Comparison is destructive to your five-year-old because their subconscious will remember it. The lie of "I am not good enough" can easily be in the head of your child for a lifetime. Think of comparison as the opposite of contentment. It will subconsciously undermine your child's happiness and cause them to struggle with a sense of unease, pain, jealousy, resentment, or anger.

On top of that, comparing the performance of your child to the performance of another can send the message that coming out on top is more important than what's learned through the task itself. If your child is mostly motivated by the desire to beat someone, they may miss the built-in lessons that are part of the process because they're only focused on the end result.

I encourage you to be conscious of comparison with your child. Love them unconditionally just the way they are and praise good interactions, healthy relationships, healthy learning, and healthy accomplishments. If they can feel about themselves as God does and believe they're capable, valued, and loved human beings, their confidence will not be shaken.

TEACH THEM TO LOOK THROUGH THE LENS OF GRACE

Five-year-olds need to know that it's okay to make mistakes. We're all imperfect, and mistakes are normal and inevitable in life. The important thing is not to get stuck on the mistake but to know how to get back up, learn from it, and try again. A child who believes they have God's grace can forgive themselves and others and recognize that they have a fresh start. It's the process of figuring out what went wrong and then trying again that develops wisdom, resilience, and confidence.

The confident child knows they're loved no matter what and that they're more than their mistakes. Knowing that Jesus accepts them when they fail helps them accept that failure can happen when they attempt a task. And they understand that God doesn't view them through the lens of their mistake but instead sees their whole heart, potential, and value.

Mistakes and failure are humbling, of course, but I love that they point to our need for help, hope, and grace from a Savior. God shows His favor to people in the midst of their failings, extending His grace through Jesus. As parents, we need to show our kids how to lean into God at this early age and view themselves and this world through the lens of God's goodness and grace. We can do that by helping them grow in their faith, reading the Bible together with them, talking about Jesus's heart and character, and making sure they have the freedom to seek.

As impressive as your five-year-old is, try not to expect more from them than they're capable of at this age, and make sure they know that you have a positive assessment of them. Parents can easily be hypercritical of their children, not realizing that their words or nonverbal communication are communicating disappointment. Your child could subconsciously process this, feel stress or anxiety from it, start to people-please, or take on perfectionistic tendencies that aren't healthy. The subconscious mind remembers both truths and lies, so be positive, genuine, truthful, and kind with your child. Communicate to them that they are cherished, that they are enough, that mistakes can be blessings, and that God sees them at their fullest potential and will be faithful to complete the good work He already started in them.

I encourage you to enjoy this special year of your child's life. We often feel sentimental as parents when we see how quickly our kids are growing. But with that growth comes even more of a glimpse of the amazing human being that God created like no one else. With your love, guidance, and prayers, your child is becoming more capable, more aware, and more confident and independent.

PRAYER

Lord, this world often tries to tell us we're not good enough and that we must live a false life of comparison. Please help us to be content with how you made us. Help us to teach our children that they are deeply loved by you and by their parents. Fill them with authentic confidence loaded with kindness and grace. In your name I pray. Amen.

Chapter 6

AGE SIX: COMPLEX BIG-KID STUFF

<hr>

"For I know the plans I have for you," declares the Lord, "plans
for welfare and not for evil, to give you a future and a hope."

—Jeremiah 29:11 (ESV)

When you see your child growing up so quickly before your
eyes, it can be simultaneously exciting and scary. Their baby
stage probably feels like it was just yesterday, and yet when you consider how much they've developed and how much you've learned,
you realize God has blessed and carried you through a lot. Your little
one is now a six-year-old ready to enter the elementary years.

Around this age, parents can start to get overly focused on the
future and forget to live in the moment with their child. This is especially the case when their six-year-old enters this new stage of life that

involves school, other older kids, and a different set of influences. Their child will be learning to solve many more complex problems and be introduced to new life situations that we can't always be present for or protect them from.

Each year your child grows, it presents you, as a parent, with an opportunity to trust God and let go a little more. This is not to say that we stop protecting and providing for them or love them any less. They're still only six. But it does means, rather, that we recognize that to love them well and raise them to be healthy, happy, confident humans, we must let them grow in independence, spread their wings a little more, and have opportunities to practice what we've been teaching them all along. This is not easy for us. It's a sacrifice and requires wisdom, discernment, and trust to do it right. But when we want what's best for our kids and care deeply about their welfare, we stand back, stay nearby, and give our kids some room to figure out the big-kid stuff.

Jeremiah 29:11 says that God has a plan for both you and your children. Not only does he have a plan, but He has also known it since the beginning of time and prepared the path for you all along. He knows exactly what this year of your child's life will be like, and He knows exactly what you child will think and feel every step of the way. He is above all, in all, and for all, and that includes your own child's heart.

As parents, we can find hope and encouragement in this verse. I know I did. Your child will face challenges, trials, and tribulations this year and throughout their life. That's the reality of living in the world. But we can prepare our child by helping them know that God is with them and has their best interests at heart. His plans are for their welfare, their happiness, their mental and emotional health, their peace, their well-being, their overall success. This verse says that He knows the future and hope He's giving them.

It's so easy to get wrapped up in worry about our child's future. Again, I know I did. These are normal feelings to have as a parent, and our concerns don't just go away. But we too can trust that God cares about our welfare as parents and has our future and hope fully covered. As we walk in step with Jesus, His plans are for our happiness, our mental and emotional health, our peace, our well-being, and our ability to be successful as parents. God knows how to make you a good parent, and even more, how to use parenting to refine and grow you to be the person He's always created you to be.

So in this year of your child's life, as they experience new emotions and new challenges, trust Him to guide you both through. I pray, along with offering the insights and ideas in this chapter, that you'll feel more equipped to help your child approach the experiences of this year with hope and confidence.

Six-Year-Old Brain Activity: Fantasy to Reality

Turning six will almost certainly convince your child that they are in the big leagues. They'll be maturing a lot this year and will want to be treated like a big kid during this stage, so statements you make or rules you have in place that make them feel younger will not go over as well. They'll still want your love and reassurance as they always have, but they'll also, a moment later, act like they're too old for these.

They know they have different thoughts, ideas, and opinions, and they can tell they've grown bigger physically. They have greater mental capacity for understanding increasingly more complex nuances, and this makes the way they want to operate in conversations a little different. This year, according to one parenting resource, "they move from being preschoolers into middle childhood, from a life dominated by fantasy to one that is beginning to be governed by logic and reason. They start to see themselves as more autonomous individuals, capable of basic independent problem solving." Your child, it continues, will start to notice that there seems to be a "right" way of doing things.[1] You'll notice your six-year-old, therefore, making tweaks to the way they do things from time to time.

A NEW WAY TO PLAY

In previous years, your child mostly used their imagination when they played, enjoying make-believe worlds where they could pretend, experiment, and explore. In this new stage of development, there will be more of a boundary between fantasy and reality in their play, and you'll see a leaning toward reality for the first time. This doesn't mean they'll necessarily stop playing pretend. Playtime is still crucial for the healthy development of a child, and your six-year-old will find their own new way to do it.

Their social development will also begin to be molded through playtime sessions with friends. They may, on occasion, even prefer to play with friends more than playing by themselves. Either way, allow them to choose what they prefer and direct their own play, so they'll be able to get out of it what they need.

THE DIGITAL AGE

Screen time will be even more relevant to your child at this age too. As mentioned in Chapter 2, one of your jobs as a parent is to establish healthy patterns and habits for your child, which includes monitoring their screen time closely. This year, with a growing awareness of the use of digital devices in our world, your child may need you to discuss any updated rules and guidelines around screen time as well as to hear your thoughts on the correct mindset around this. You may need to set new limits now that your child is older and even engage in your child's screen time yourself.

I highly recommend setting parental locks on any devices, so the vast world of the internet will not be at their fingertips 24/7. There are countless stories of unsupervised kids surfing the internet freely, purchasing items on Amazon with the saved credit cards on file, or finding themselves viewing harmful or inappropriate content on websites. Our kids have a whole new set of challenges to face as they grow up, and during this time when they're still so young, they lack the maturity, discernment, and life experience that's needed to navigate the complex digital world. We as parents need to be aware of this digital age as we set healthy parameters for our children to follow and help them make smart choices.

FEELINGS

Because their understanding of the world is expanding rapidly this year, some six-year-olds have feelings of fear or apprehension. The thought of starting school alone can introduce them to new anxieties and insecurities. But this also brings more opportunities for healthy teaching moments and good connection between you and your child.

Help them to always stay grounded in the love of Jesus and the fact that He is their ultimate protector and provider, there whenever they need him. The psalms contain some comforting words of truth, and you can always read some with your child to encourage them. It's important to make sure your little one knows that feelings of fear or anxiety are perfectly normal and that they don't need to worry about having the feelings or emotions themselves. But God tells them that He's bigger than their worries, and they don't have to be controlled by them or to dwell in them.

You may see a little more of a push and pull with feelings this year. At this age, your child's feelings are still freely flowing, but the way your child thinks about and copes with challenges is affected by their growing ability to apply logic and reason. On one hand, they have real, raw emotions, and on the other hand, their brains now provide them with a different way to reason. Remind your child that even when they feel conflicted or pulled in opposite directions, He is the anchor in the storms that life naturally brings our way. Your little one will need all kinds of reminders, encouragement, and support because it will sometimes be hard for them to know what their feelings are telling them. You can help them identify their emotions in a healthy way. Identifying and addressing their feelings can provide language for making a situation more manageable for your child. The goal will be to soothe their feelings, help them regulate their emotions, and build their confidence.

Confidence Building Blocks

As mentioned, this year for your child will be full of new experiences, but these experiences will bring about new challenges and risks. Your task this year is to allow your child to take on some of these challenges and risks on their own. Doing this will provide them with opportunities to problem solve, make decisions, and become more responsible. As they learn through these challenges, they'll come to see and believe that they are capable and resilient, and their sense of confidence and self-worth will increase.

Consider some of the following confidence-building tips for your family as you support your child through their new experiences.

HELP THEM PERSEVERE

During this year, it will be doubly as important for you to allow your child to learn some things on their own. When the process doesn't go smoothly or they don't get the results they were hoping for, your child may react negatively, expressing anger or disappointment or feeling badly about themselves.

As a parent, you can offer them support or encouragement, but I recommend still making sure your child knows they have the power to decide what happens next. Rather than stepping in to solve the problem, you'll want to cultivate in your child the kind of grit they need to do hard things and persevere. We all hate to see our children floundering, struggling, or feeling pain, but if we remove their ability to learn and grow through adversity, we do them a disservice because they won't have the skills they need to handle the next problem.

Teaching your child the importance of perseverance is part of their journey of independence. They can't grow into a healthy adult without it because it's a key factor in a person's ability to be successful, resilient, and confident. Let your child know that it's okay to feel frustrated and sometimes, failures are a blessing.

To encourage your child to pick themselves up, take a new perspective, and try again, you can share stories about your own personal experiences with failure or mistakes. Let your child know how you felt at the time and what you did to change the situation. You can also share stories of others' experiences. There are many inspiring stories of people who chose not to give up in adversity, rose above difficult circumstances, and made a difference in the world.

I'll add that persevering doesn't mean your child always has to try again no matter what. There are important lessons to learn about a positive, solutions-oriented mindset, but in some circumstances, it's absolutely okay to quit. You can help your child see how they're capable in all sorts of ways. There's no need to force a particular situation if it seems counterproductive. The goal is to raise a happy, healthy, confident child who understands their self-worth and is excited about the world of possibilities before them.

ADDRESS YOUR PAST HURTS

To be able to move confidently and capably into the world, we sometimes need to recognize how pain or disappointments from our past color our present. Our subconscious remembers low self-worth, heartbreak, regret, and unforgiveness, and though we have a new beginning from God every day because of His grace, some wounds we've been carrying have a hard time healing. God understands this and wants to alleviate our pain.

To raise an authentically confident child, we sometimes need to take a look at ourselves to see where we may be stuck on aspects of our past. Even if we function just fine in everyday life, painfulness we experienced and ways of coping still inform the way we parent. The impatience we feel, harsh words that come out of our mouths, rules we set, and advice we give are in many ways influenced by what our subconscious selves remember. Is it more of a pet peeve than it should be when someone forgets to turn off a light, arrives at an event late, or can't control their emotions? To be the best parents we can be for our child, we may need to address our past hurts. Doing this will also help us avoid making some of the same mistakes with our kids or causing them to feel badly about things that have little to do with them.

You may have heard the saying "Hurt people hurt people." I believe this is true when it comes to parenting. If you have low self-esteem and lack confidence because of past hurts, it will be extra challenging to raise your child to be confident and feel worthy. According to parenting site Ask Dr. Sears, "A child's self-esteem is acquired, not inherited. Certain parenting traits and certain character traits, such as anger and fearfulness, are learned in each generation."[2] I believe we need to focus on our own hearts first before we can do a great job as parents, but if we do the hard work of addressing what we need to, we can break the cycle with our kids.

Healing from old wounds takes a lot of prayer, wise counsel, and support. Many people seek the help of a trained therapist, licensed counselor, or pastor, and there's enormous value in this. Part of the process of healing involves forgiving those who wronged us, so we may overcome feelings of bitterness, resentment, or disappointment. Our subconscious draws us back again and again to those negative states, sometimes when we don't even fully recognize it, and then it feels like the harm is perpetuated again and again. If you can forgive your parents or those who hurt you, they will no longer be able to control your thoughts, feelings, and actions. Forgiving them doesn't excuse the offense itself, but it allows you to release it and be free to move on. My book *Fear Not* offers some guidance in this area too.

Healing is a process, but I encourage you to pursue it for your child if you need to. Ask God what you should address and how to go about it. Pray that He would touch you in all the hurt places of your heart and help you find peace. And ask Him to protect and show favor to your child, so they would not need to experience the effects of someone else's sin. They—and you—are beloved in God's sight. He sees your pain, will be faithful to heal and help you, and desires to bring you to a place of authentic confidence in Him.

ENCOURAGE GROWTH AND MATURITY

Many of the confidence-building suggestions discussed in earlier chapters overlap between the stages of development. The healthy benefits and life lessons a child receives by engaging in play, taking on different responsibilities, and communing with God are applicable when they are six as well. In this section, I briefly return to them, with some six-year-old-specific tips to show you how incorporating these into everyday life with your child will continue to encourage them toward growth and maturity and ultimately, greater confidence.

Play

Your six-year-old will play individually and with friends more this year, traversing between the worlds of fantasy and reality as they do. It's important to give them room to do this, so they can learn the lessons from these that they need to. This doesn't negate your presence at other times, however. Active engagement is still crucial, and your child needs dedicated time to play with you too. The times may be shorter, perhaps for ten to fifteen minutes at a stretch, or your child may want to spend a whole afternoon with you one day. Follow their lead and let them direct the play when you can. The point is to go into their world.

During play, you may pick up on real feelings or emotions they're experiencing in other facets of their life. Different fears or insecurities that come with this age may surface in the middle of a game. Remember that your child is still learning how to communicate with you, and it could be that the easiest way for them to express the things that are challenging to them is to do it indirectly through play. Spending time with your child, especially through play, will allow you to have your finger more on the pulse of their mental and emotional health.

Responsibilities

Don't be afraid or hesitant to assign a little more responsibility around the house, either. Your child may have homework now that they're in first grade, but it's still a good idea to allow them to continue to help you around the house and build on skills they've developed over time. Six-year-olds still generally like to please their parents, so your child may be perfectly happy to do chores, especially if you introduce some newer, more challenging ones because your child has demonstrated themselves to be capable. Giving your child tasks and responsibilities communicates to them that you trust them, which helps build their self-esteem and makes them feel more confident. If the specific chores or tasks are part of the regular routine, you're also creating healthy patterns and habits in your family that allow your child to become increasingly more responsible and confident.

Faith

Most importantly, continue to journey in faith with your six-year-old, pointing them to Jesus. The analogy of thinking about a young child's brain as a sponge is still very much in play here. If you establish healthy habits of prayer and Bible time while they're young, they'll always have a foundation of truth, hope, love, and encouragement as they grow. You don't need to force this on your child, and you can approach this recognizing that only God's spirit can make His truth take hold in your child's heart. Especially now that your six-year-old's brain can handle conversations that are more complex, give them all the room they need to ask questions about God's character and His desire for people's lives. Also, model for your child what it looks like to live a life in tune with His Spirit. Over time, your child will feel more confident and more loved if they feel that the God of the universe adores them and will always take care of them.

May God bless you with great wisdom as you raise your big kid this year. He has an amazing plan for you and your family, and I hope you will find peace, help, and joy as you apply some of the suggestions I mentioned here.

PRAYER

God, my goal is to give my child more independence and less control as I transition from the role of a protector to teacher and coach. Help me to understand what I need to raise a big kid and help them thrive. I pray that you would lead me to the knowledge necessary to anticipate my child's changes and always respond with love, patience, and guidance filled with grace. Please help me to walk closely with you, seeking strength, inspiration, and confidence from you to become the best parent I can be for my six-year-old. In Christ's name, amen.

Chapter 7

AGE SEVEN: MOVING MOUNTAINS

For truly, I say to you, if you have faith like a grain of mustard seed, you will say to this mountain, "Move from here to there," and it will move, and nothing will be impossible for you.

—Matthew 17:20 (ESV)

There are many mountains we face as parents. With your child turning seven now, I know you've climbed a few of them already. Making it up even just one of those mountains took great strength, stamina, and mental and emotional toughness, and you undoubtedly were tired or struggled at points along the way. You found your footing, built your endurance, and enjoyed different views as you went. You're more experienced now and know a lot more about climbing, but you can see on the horizon beyond this year that there are still mountains ahead.

Life is full of them, some bigger than others, and how you take them on is what matters the most for you and your family. When challenges arise with parenting, let God help you with the mountains. Matthew 17 says that if your faith is as big as even a mustard seed—a seed that's about the size of a grain of sand—then anything is possible. What a wonderful God we have who tells us that if we have even just a speck of faith, He gives what we need to take on the entire mountain so that it no longer feels like an obstacle to us.

During their year of being seven (where has the time gone?!), your child is definitely a big kid, and this stage of development has its own unique challenges and joys. Your child's individuality is shining even more, and they're able to express their individuality better than ever before. You and your spouse may see aspects of your personalities or habits—both good and bad—in your child's behavior.

In the meantime, your seven-year-old's rapidly developing brain has still been soaking up as much information as it can, including experiences and perspectives learned in school and from other external influences. This year is about building up your child, so they can learn to move any mountains they need to in their life. With confidence, faith, and your continuous loving support, nothing will be impossible for them.

Seven-Year-Old Brain Activity: The Great Impression

Because of the significant emotional and mental changes taking place in your child's brain around this age, they are absorbing most everything around them both consciously and unconsciously. I think of this year as one in which all the different influences in your child's life are making a big impression on their brain. They'll carry these impressions into the coming years.

Education.com notes that when a child hits the age of seven, their brain's "frontal and temporal lobes, which control cognitive functions, grow enormously—more than at any other time in a person's life. And at the same time, these lobes are making neural connections with the system that controls emotions. In other words, both thinking and feeling get a major overhaul."[1] Though your child has already been developing in some of these areas little by little, there's a notable change around this year when they're capable of so much more. In terms of cognitive advancements, they're able to use language in a more complex way, and you'll see their verbal communication, reading skills, and writing skills improve. Emotionally, they're beginning to handle feelings better and know how to communicate about these to others, though this sometimes exhibits differently in boys and girls, with girls generally maturing more quickly in this area and seeming to be more in touch with their feelings.

Your seven-year-old is also experiencing changes to areas of their brain that affect relationship-building and connection. You'll see your child, around this time, begin to place more importance on friendships. Because of school, they will have more friends to play with and may even have a "best friend" around this age as well. As a parent, you'll see that you are no longer the only influence over your child, and though you may still be the main voice they hear and follow right now, they do have other influences that affect their decision making. You can pray that God gives your child good friends, ones who are positive influences. You can also talk with your child about the qualities of a good friend and let your child know that you expect them to be a good friend to others.

Among all the other changes, your child begins to develop a sense of morality around the age of seven. In previous years, your child may not have understood why playing with the expensive glassware from the cabinet would get them in trouble. They just knew not to do it because they were told not to do it. But now, they're capable of understanding why they were instructed in the way they were, so if they choose to disobey, it could be that they've done it knowingly and willingly. Their sense of justice, right and wrong, and good and bad will be sharper than in previous years.

As mentioned, you'll also notice big changes with their sense of individuality around this time. They'll let you know their likes with clothing, food, people, and activities. It will be much more obvious, for example, which activities they really enjoy. You may see them requesting to paint, draw, sing, play soccer, do parkour, or even write stories. And you'll know this because they'll be motivated to suggest and spend time in the activity themselves.

With all the new developments with your seven-year-old, what are some ways you can guide and support them in this stage so that they become more authentically confident?

Confidence Building Blocks

During this middle childhood phase with your child, they'll want to exercise their growing independence but will still be looking to you for your encouragement and advice. Guiding them toward confidence at this stage will require you to focus on key areas that are important to them right now: the activities they enjoy, their life at school, and their friendships.

ENCOURAGE THEIR PASSIONS

As mentioned earlier, your seven-year-old will have likes and dislikes that are unique to them. They will be excited about certain things, and these things will offer insights about who they are and what matters to them. As parents, we would do well to observe these in our kids and consider how we might support our child in areas they're passionate about. When we look at our child for who they are and what they're interested in, we can help them blossom into who they want to be.

Parents sometimes have the notion that interests and passions their kids have now might be indicators of things they pursue later in life. This could be, but child and adolescent psychotherapist Katie Hurley points out that "passion isn't a life sentence. It can shift and change as kids grow."[2] We should be there to support, encourage, and guide our child with things they're interested in, and be prepared to do the same if those interests shift.

I'll throw out a gentle warning to parents who want their child to participate in a particular activity that the parent may like but the child does not. Many activities like this are worth pursuing, and some of them you may insist on for your child's good. Sometimes, a child rejects the idea of an activity simply because they don't yet know what it entails. Other times, certain activities, like reading, piano, or basketball, require practice, which is not necessarily fun to a child after their initial interest has worn off. If the activity has merit, it's not unreasonable that you might ask you child to stick with it. But I note this because it is different than also allowing your child to do things they're excited about. If you have them do an activity they don't want to do, make sure you add one in they do.

If you can tell your child is deeply unhappy about continuing an activity, consider if it's worth the cost of discounting their feelings. As a more extreme example, I'd guess that not all little girls enjoy participating in beauty pageants, as I've seen on television shows when the stakes and the stress are high for the child, and parents have made the pageants more about themselves. I mention this, so you can be sensitive to the way your child may be trying to express their individuality through their likes. If an activity just isn't working, and they feel like their voice isn't being heard, it may be a good idea to table it, at least for a little while, so they can explore another activity they have more passion for. When your child is intrinsically motivated to do an activity, they will benefit from it much more than an activity they don't really want to do. As parents, we don't want to tear our child's confidence down or only force our own goals on them.

I encourage you to also take the opportunity to grow with your child, engaging with them in their areas of interest. My wife and I used to take our kids to science museums, historical forts, and other interactive places where we could all learn together, have fun, and make memories. At home, you can read and discuss books together with your child about subjects they're interested in. If they like to paint, paint with them. If they love soccer, kick a ball around with them. Through these experiences together, they will naturally grow more confident when they know you support them, care about their interests, and appreciate them for who they are.

BE INVOLVED IN THEIR SCHOOL LIFE

Your seven-year-old will also be consumed with their school life at this age. It takes up a large part of their day, and there are many influences there that are helping shape their thoughts, opinions, and interests. It can be mentally stimulating, challenging, inspiring, and fun. It can also be a place that harms your child's confidence and self-esteem. If your child perceives that many other kids are better at something than they are, for example, they may struggle with how this makes them feel. They may not know that this is normal and a part of learning. But with your support and understanding, they can gain perspective, grow, and do and feel better.

Your child isn't around you for much of the day, so show them some extra love and attention after school if you're able to. Some kids need to decompress a little and aren't ready to share all the details about their day. That's okay. If they know you care and are interested, that still makes all the difference. You can have a conversation with them when they're ready, perhaps over dinner or at bedtime. And the love and support you want to offer them can take on different shapes. Regardless, try to listen well to what your child says, read emails and handouts that come home from school, notice how your child talks about friends or homework, and connect with their teacher if you need to. If they seem to be facing a tough situation, be supportive and offer suggestions, but let them take the lead with coming up with solutions to the problem. Don't worry if you don't have the right answers or know exactly what to say. Your child simply needs to know you're there, available, and open, and they'll have more confidence to work through their complex feelings.

GUIDE THEM IN THEIR FRIENDSHIPS

When it comes to their social life, a lot of the same approaches can be applied. As parents, we want our children to flourish and be accepted and loved by everyone. But unfortunately, we have sin in the world, and people can be selfish, dismissive, unkind, or downright mean. If you sense that your child is having a hard time making friends at school or is feeling lonely and disconnected, show them empathy, listen to them, offer them your thoughts and advice, and touch base with their teacher if necessary. A teacher can create opportunities in the classroom for kids to work together or watch the different interactions during recess. Outside of school, you can see if your child might be open to activities where they can connect with like-minded kids.

If you sense there is any bullying going on, it's important to step in and let the teacher know, so they can intervene at school and help with confidence and self-esteem. Tony Volk, an associate professor of child and youth studies at Brock University, says that "For a kid who is being bullied, having a close friend can cut in half the long-term risks of mental health problems, such as anxiety or depression. Intervention from a teacher or another adult can also decrease the long-term risk that the child or youth's self-esteem is affected."[3]

At home, empathy and compassion will be important tools. Jesus demonstrated empathy and compassion throughout His ministry. You won't find any miraculous event that Jesus did without first showing empathy or compassion. I encourage you to follow Jesus's example, continuously and intentionally extending empathy and compassion to your child. Comfort them, pray for them, encourage them to stand up for themselves, and guide them toward authentic confidence. And make sure you listen well. The more aware you are of the situation, the better you can help your child. Hopefully, bullying is never an issue for your child, but you can also teach them what to do if they see it happening to someone else.

With your support, your seven-year-old can learn how to begin to navigate friendships and school interactions. It's a big part of their life this year, so paying attention to what they say and how they feel about friends can help you know what they need. You can offer advice, set up playdates, invite their friends to attend activities with your child. The goal is to allow them to develop healthy friendships and have positive connections that help them grow and become happier and more confident.

I pray this book has encouraged you and given you hope along the way that you are a worthy parent and not alone on the journey. I know parenting is a challenge, but to me, raising a child who is authentically confident, joyful in who they are, and full of God's love is one of the greatest gifts we can offer the world. We have the honor and privilege of pouring love into an amazing, uniquely made human being and helping them become all God created them to be. With the confidence we instill in them and faith and trust in God, they'll be able to climb and conquer any of life's mountains, and nothing will be impossible to them.

PRAYER

God, I pray for my child's continued growth and the wisdom I need to raise them to be authentically confident, capable, and independent. Please allow me to cast away doubts, fears, insecurities, failings, and old strongholds I have so that they do not become my child's. Lead me to a daily conversation full of love and gratitude with you, Lord. Help me always to teach your infinite love and have me walk in that love all the time. Please give me your Holy Spirit to guide my child and me today and forevermore. In Jesus's name, amen.

CONCLUSION: NEXT STEPS

Consider this book the first step on your journey to becoming a spectacular, confidence-building parent. I hope that the insights and information in it have blessed and enriched you and you feel more confident about bringing your child through the different developmental stages not only now but also in the years beyond the first eight. I hope also that the truths I share about how God feels about you, your child, and your family will help you in moments when you need them and elevate every situation.

You can return to individual chapters as you prepare for your child's birthday each year, rereading sections to refresh your memory and find advice and encouragement for the coming year. As I mention at one point, my wife and I committed to reading age-specific parenting books for our sons every year of their life as they were growing, and the help we received from these was invaluable. I invite you to do the same or find good help through the countless parenting resources available online as well. See what works best for your family, figure out which tips you want to apply, and continue to do this until your child is headed to college.

It makes a world of difference when you feel more confident and prepared to help your child through all the experiences they have ahead, including body changes, peer pressure, drugs and alcohol, sex, dating, healthy relationships, first jobs, thinking about the future, and applying to college. I'm just one voice among many, but I think you have at your disposal countless strategies to help positively influence your child to make good decisions throughout their childhood—decisions that bear weight on the rest of their lives. You'll also be better prepared for the challenges, disappointments, and rejections that inevitably come with all these changes.

I pray that you'll have all you need to love your child no matter what and to laugh your way through the natural changes in their personalities. I pray that you'll learn and grow, becoming the best version of yourself as you parent the child God has given to you. And I pray that your child and the experience of loving them brings you great joy. May the Lord always give you His wisdom, knowledge, and grace to be great at your most important job: raising an authentically confident child. Amen!

ACKNOWLEDGMENTS

I thank and acknowledge you for taking the time to study being an awesome parent. The fact that you care enough to use this book as a guide and influence on your parenting gives me great joy. I think you are amazing for doing the work to be better at your most important job: raising the children God has entrusted to you. Please tell your friends and family about your journey of learning to be a great parent.

I thank my staff, editors, and Greenleaf publishing team. Special thanks go to my assistant, Lisa West; my prepublishing editor, Matt Kuvakos; and my publishing editor, Jessica Choi. They all really poured their parenting hearts into this work, and for them I am truly grateful.

I am really thankful for the good work of my parents—especially my father, for importing the values of the Lord in me. He pointed out that he and my mother were not perfect, but they both loved us. My father expressed a sincere desire for us to emulate the good of my parents and forgive and let go of the mistakes, most of which were unintentional.

My oldest sister, Mary, who, being nine years older, filled my subconscious mind with kindness and love for her little brother and modeled how to succeed as an executive and successful businessperson at a time when that was very difficult to maneuver in a man's business world.

I thank my superstar parenting partner and wife, Ann. Together we worked really hard to be the best parents we could be. We forwent material items early in our lives together to save money and prioritize our boy's education and spiritual growth. We tried to model love, faith, generosity, hard work, and intentionality.

I thank my sons, Alex and Jacob. I am grateful for their relationship and love and for their authentic confidence and willingness to be intentional and teachable. I also thank them for their grace and forgiveness when we, as parents, did not model well.

Most importantly, I thank God, who loves us all, for His love, truth, grace, and beauty.

NOTES

Introduction

1. Cleve W. Stevens, *The Best in Us: People, Profit, and the Remaking of Modern Leadership* (New York: Beaufort Books, 2012).

Chapter 1

1. Adam & Mila, "Brain Development of Children from 0–6 years—Facts Every Parent Should Know," accessed January 18, 2022, https://www.adam-mila.com/brain-development-children-0-6-years/.

2. Judith Graham and Leslie A. Forstadt, "Bulletin #4356: Children and Brain Development: What We Know about How Children Learn," University of Maine, 2011, https://extension.umaine.edu/publications/4356e/.

3. Raising Children Network (Australia), "0–1 Month: Newborn Development," accessed March 13, 2020, https://raisingchildren.net.au/newborns/development/development-tracker/0-1-month.

4. Graham and Forstadt, "Bulletin #4356: Children and Brain Development."

5. Harvard University Center on the Developing Child, "Brain Architecture," accessed March 1, 2022, https://developingchild.harvard.edu/science/key-concepts/brain-architecture/.

6. Julie Greicius, "The Benefits of Touch for Babies, Parents," Stanford Medicine, September 23, 2013, https://med.stanford.edu/news/all -news/2013/09/the-benefits-of-touch-for-babies-parents.html.

7. Centers for Disease Control and Prevention, "Early Brain Development and Health," March 25, 2022, https://www.cdc.gov/ncbddd/childdevelopment/ early-brain-development.html.

8. "Babies Exposed to Stimulation Get Brain Boost," *ScienceDaily*, January 2, 2017, https://www.sciencedaily.com/releases/2017/01/170102143458.htm.

9. Kimmie Fink, "7 Ways Your Baby Is Trying to Say They Feel Safe," *Romper*, May 7, 2018, https://www.romper.com/p/7-ways-your-baby-is-trying-to-say -they-feel-safe-8992008.

10. Jacqueline Burt Wang, "Why Is Routine Important for Babies?" *Parents*, October 3, 2005, https://www.parents.com/baby/care/newborn/why-is -routine-important-for-babies/.

11. Zero to Three, "Developing Self-Confidence from Birth to 12 Months," May 19, 2016, https://www.zerotothree.org/resources/1284-developing-self -confidence-from-birth-to-12-months.

12. Karl Eller, *Integrity Is All You've Got: And Seven Other Lessons of the Entrepreneurial Life* (New York: McGraw-Hill, 2004).

Chapter 2

1. Rishi Sriram, "Why Ages 2–7 Matter So Much for Brain Development," *Edutopia*, June 24, 2020, https://www.edutopia.org/article/why-ages -2-7-matter-so-much-brain-development.

2. Stanford Children's Health, "The Growing Child: 2-Year-Olds," accessed February 2, 2022, https://www.stanfordchildrens.org/en/topic/ default?id=the-growing-child-2-year-olds-90-P02303.

3. Brooke Junior, "Play Skills Checklist for Toddlers and Preschoolers," Behavior Place, January 20, 2020, https://behaviorplace.com/tips/play-skills -checklist-for-toddlers-and-preschoolers.

4. Pamela Li, "Importance of Play in Early Childhood (9 Benefits & Infographic)," *Parenting for Brain*, March 22, 2022, https://www.parenting forbrain.com/benefits-play-learning-activities-early-childhood/.

5. UNICEF Parenting, "Your Toddler's Developmental Milestones at 2 Years," accessed February 3, 2022, https://www.unicef.org/parenting/child -development/your-toddlers-developmental-milestones-2-years.

6. PennState Extension, "Developing Memory," 2016, https://extension.psu .edu/programs/betterkidcare/early-care/tip-pages/all/developing-memory.

7. Jenny Des Jarlais, "How to Nurture Your 2-Year-Old's Imagination," *BabyCenter*, accessed February 3, 2022, https://www.babycenter.com/child/ development/how-to-nurture-your-2-year-olds-imagination_64144.

8. Jay L. Hoecker, "I've Heard a Lot about the Terrible Twos: Why Are 2-Year-Olds So Difficult?" Mayo Clinic, February 23, 2022, https://www .mayoclinic.org/healthy-lifestyle/infant-and-toddler-health/expert-answers/ terrible-twos/faq-20058314.

9. Stanford Children's Health, "Age-Appropriate Speech and Language Milestones," accessed February 12, 2021, https://www.stanfordchildrens.org/ en/topic/default?id=age-appropriate-speech-and-language-milestones -90-P02170.

10. *Evan Almighty*, dir. Tom Shadyac (Universal Pictures, 2007), DVD.

11. Sarah Henry, "How to Build Your Preschooler's Self-Esteem," *BabyCenter*, accessed February 23, 2021, https://www.babycenter.com/child/ development/how-to-build-your-preschoolers-self-esteem_64036.

12. Liz Greene, "4 Small Ways to Build Confidence in Kids," Child Mind Institute, accessed February 24, 2021, https://childmind.org/article/4-small -ways-to-build-confidence-in-kids/.

13. "12 Ways to Raise a Confident Child," *Ask Dr. Sears*, accessed May 28, 2021, https://www.askdrsears.com/topics/parenting/child-rearing-and -development/12-ways-help-your-child-build-self-confidence/.

14. Montessori Academy, "Repetition and Child Development in Montessori Education," accessed February 7, 2022, https://montessoriacademy.com.au/ repetition-child-development-montessori/.

15. Sonia Livingstone, "How Young Children Are Using the Internet," World Economic Forum, October 9, 2015, https://www.weforum.org/agenda/2015/10/how-young-children-are-using-the-internet/.

16. Michelle Roberts, "Screen Time 'May Harm Toddlers,'" *BBC News*, January 28, 2019, https://www.bbc.com/news/health-47026834.

17. American Academy of Child and Adolescent Psychiatry, "Screen Time and Children," February 2020, https://www.aacap.org/AACAP/Families_and_Youth/Facts_for_Families/FFF-Guide/Children-And-Watching-TV-054.aspx.

18. Jill Christensen, "Children and Screen Time: How Much Is Too Much?" Mayo Clinic Health System, May 28, 2021, https://www.mayoclinichealthsystem.org/hometown-health/speaking-of-health/children-and-screen-time.

19. Steven Reinberg, "Too Much Screen Time May Stunt Toddlers' Brains," *WebMD*, November 5, 2019, https://www.webmd.com/children/news/20191105/too-much-screen-time-may-be-stunting-toddlers-brains.

20. Roberts, "Screen Time 'May Harm Toddlers.'"

Chapter 3

1. Patricia McBroom, "In the New Science of Children's Minds, Babies Are Smarter Than Adults, according to Book Co-authored by UC Berkeley Psychologist," University of California, Berkeley, August 10, 1999, https://www.berkeley.edu/news/media/releases/99legacy/8-10-1999.html.

2. Stanford Children's Health, "The Growing Child: 3-Year-Olds," accessed February 9, 2022, https://www.stanfordchildrens.org/en/topic/default?id=the-growing-child-3-year-olds-90-P02296.

3. First Things First, "Brain Development," accessed February 10, 2022, https://www.firstthingsfirst.org/early-childhood-matters/brain-development/.

4. Cheryl Flanders, "Why, Why, Why Are Some 3-Year-Olds Always Asking 'Why'?" KinderCare, March 2017, https://www.kindercare.com/content-hub/articles/2017/march/why-why-why-do-some-3yearolds-ask-why-all-the-time.

5. Patrick Sauer, "What's Going On Inside a Toddler's Brain, according to Science," *Fatherly*, September 26, 2016, https://www.fatherly.com/health -science/toddler-brain-neurology/.

6. Harvard Health Publishing, "Giving Thanks Can Make You Happier," August 14, 2021, https://www.health.harvard.edu/healthbeat/giving-thanks -can-make-you-happier.

7. Amber Dance, "Making and Breaking Connections in the Brain," *Knowable Magazine*, August 18, 2020, https://knowablemagazine.org/article/health -disease/2020/what-does-a-synapse-do.

8. Kenneth R. Ginsburg, "The Importance of Play in Promoting Healthy Child Development and Maintaining Strong Parent-Child Bonds," *Pediatrics* 119, no. 1 (January 2007), https://doi.org/10.1542/peds.2006-2697.

9. Zero to Three, "Developing Self-Confidence from 24–36 Months," May 19, 2010, https://www.zerotothree.org/resources/1292-developing -self-confidence-from-24-36-months.

Chapter 4

1. T. T. Brown and T. L. Jernigan, "Brain Development during the Preschool Years," *Neuropsychology Review* 22 (December 2012), https://doi.org/ 10.1007/s11065-012-9214-1.

2. Child Mind Institute, "Complete Guide to Developmental Milestones," accessed July 1, 2020, https://childmind.org/guide/parents-guide-to -developmental-milestones/#block_882b131b-4ed8-40cf-ac11 -4831e17ef7a4.

3. Raising Children Network (Australia), "4–5 years: Preschooler Development," March 17, 2022, https://raisingchildren.net.au/preschoolers/ development/development-tracker/4-5-years.

4. Katy Abel, "Children's Development of Spirituality," *FamilyEducation*, accessed February 12, 2022, https://www.familyeducation.com/life/social -emotional-development/childrens-development-spirituality.

5. Susan A. Miller, "Ages and Stages: How Children Adjust to School, 3–4; 'I'll Bring My Duckie,'" *Scholastic*, accessed April 7, 2021, https://www.scholastic.com/teachers/articles/teaching-content/ages-stages-how-children-adjust-school/.

Chapter 5

1. First Things First, "Brain Development," accessed February 13, 2022, https://www.firstthingsfirst.org/early-childhood-matters/brain-development/.

2. Hank Pellissier, "Inside the Kindergartner's Brain," GreatSchools, July 6, 2016, https://www.greatschools.org/gk/articles/kindergartner-brain-development/.

3. Eddie Brummelman, Stefanie A. Nelemans, Sander Thomaes, and Bram Orobio de Castro, "When Parents' Praise Inflates, Children's Self-Esteem Deflates," *Child Development* 88, no. 6 (August 2017): 1799–1809.

4. Gwen Dewar, "The Effects of Praise: 7 Evidence-Based Tips for Using Praise Wisely," *Parenting Science*, 2019, https://parentingscience.com/effects-of-praise.

Chapter 6

1. Michelle Anthony, "Cognitive Development in 6–7 Year Olds," *Scholastic Parents*, accessed February 14, 2022, https://www.scholastic.com/parents/family-life/creativity-and-critical-thinking/development-milestones/cognitive-development-6-7-year-olds.html.

2. "12 Ways to Raise a Confident Child," *Ask Dr. Sears*, accessed May 28, 2021, https://www.askdrsears.com/topics/parenting/child-rearing-and-development/12-ways-help-your-child-build-self-confidence/.

Chapter 7

1. "Lucky Age 7: Why and How Kids Change," *Education.com*, May 14, 2014, https://www.education.com/magazine/article/Lucky_7_How/.

2. Susan Newman, "How to Support and Nurture Your Child's Passions," *Psychology Today*, October 20, 2015, https://www.psychologytoday.com/us/blog/singletons/201510/how-support-and-nurture-your-childs-passions.

3. Antonia Mcguire, "How to Rebuild Your Child's Self-Esteem after Bullying," *Today's Parent*, July 13, 2017, https://www.todaysparent.com/kids/school-age/how-to-rebuild-your-childs-self-esteem-after-bullying/.

ABOUT THE AUTHOR

John Kaites is a pastor, husband, and father of two. He is a successful practicing attorney and entrepreneur who has owned some or all of eighteen companies. He began his career as a television news broadcaster before moving on to serve as an assistant attorney general, a state representative, and a state senator.

John is a graduate of Fuller Theological Seminary, Duquesne University School of Law, and Allegheny College. He is currently working on a master of arts in ministry from Phoenix Seminary. In addition to working in business, teaching, and practicing law, he helps pastors and churches rethink their growth strategies in an entrepreneurial and transformational way. This is John's second book. He is also the author of *Fear Not: Two Weeks of Living Boldly into God's Authentic Confidence*. You may reach John at john@johnkaitesauthor.com.